# JUST ROLL WITH IT!

## 7 Battle Tested Truths for Building a Resilient Life

SARAH PLUMMER TAYLOR

Expanded edition with
Foreword by Kate Hendricks Thomas, PhD
Afterword by David L. Albright, PhD

innovo
PUBLISHING

Published by
Innovo Publishing, LLC
www.innovopublishing.com
1-888-546-2111

Providing Full-Service Publishing Services for
Christian Authors, Artists & Organizations: Hardbacks, Paperbacks,
eBooks, Audiobooks, Music & Film

**JUST ROLL WITH IT!**
**7 BATTLE TESTED TRUTHS FOR BUILDING A RESILIENT LIFE**
Copyright © 2015 Sarah Plummer Taylor
All rights reserved.

Unless otherwise noted, Scripture is taken from THE HOLY BIBLE, NEW INTERNATIONAL VERSION®, NIV® Copyright © 1973, 1978, 1984, 2011 by Biblica, Inc.® Used by permission. All rights reserved worldwide.

Although the *Chicago Manual of Style* was used as the primary guide in the editorial decisions for this title, exceptions were made to accommodate a style more accepted in the military community.

**Some names have been changed.**

Library of Congress Control Number: 2015956157
ISBN 978-1-61314-312-4

Cover Design & Interior Layout: Innovo Publishing, LLC

Printed in the United States of America
U.S. Printing History

Third Edition: December 2015

# PRAISE FOR *JUST ROLL WITH IT!*

"Sarah Plummer Taylor's must-read book will inspire you to personal greatness, challenge you to transform absolutely every area of your life, and dare you to love the life you live! Life rarely meets our expectations, but with a positive attitude, there can be some great surprises along the way. Sarah's friendly voice will encourage you to change what you can, as she has, and then let go enough to live life resiliently and magically because sometimes, it's true, you gotta just roll."

**—Kristine Carlson, co-author of the New York Times best-selling**
*Don't Sweat the Small Stuff* **book series: In Love, for Women, for Moms**

"Sarah Plummer Taylor's *Just Roll With It!* sounds the clarion call of honesty: it asks readers to strip away the excuses we too readily feed ourselves, and instead gaze boldly at our own souls, intuition, pain, and capacity for growth. From this place of radical honesty, Sarah encourages us to take courageous and compassionate action on our own behalves— despite our imperfections. Her personal story, shared in the form of gripping narratives, is woven together with universal truths and insights that empower as much as they inspire. I imagine even casual readers will be moved and challenged, but those lucky readers who choose to take action as they learn will undoubtedly grow too. This book is a rare opportunity to get inside the head of a truly inspirational human being, and to begin or accelerate your own transformation. I recommend it highly—particularly for military service members and veterans, and especially in tandem with one of Sarah's coaching programs."

**—Lydia Davey, US Marine Veteran; co-author and course instructor**
**for UCSF's Women Warriors: Stress, Resilience, and Post-Traumatic**
**Growth**

"Sarah Plummer Taylor's book is a must read by all and a great investment to change your life for the better! Sarah provides a practical, totally comprehensive guide to owning the weather over your head and the grid square where you put your boots. I love the way Sarah uses a simple but meaningful acronym of SEMPER and turns it into a 'lifestyle' reminder that will make you feel better, look better, and have a more enjoyable life."

**—Joseph "Joe Marine" Shusko, retired Marine Corps Lieutenant Colonel and author of** *Tie-Ins for Life*

"Sarah is on to something profound, the path to personal growth after adversity through the courage to share her story and the tools that helped her find her intuitive center. She reminds us that when the journey is rough, answers come not so much through trying to figure things out, but by attending to how our experiences are stored in the body."

**—Charles W. Hoge, MD, Colonel (Ret), Author of** *Once a Warrior—Always a Warrior: Navigating the Transition from Combat to Home.*

"While Sarah's triumphs and challenges may be uniquely hers, her stories carry universal messages that resonate no matter your life experiences. As a person who has never played on an organized sports team, served in the military, nor a myriad of other experiences like those Sarah shares, I found myself surprised at how much I connected to her powerful messages. I could see my own life choices reflected in her candid, vivid, and captivating stories. Sarah's SEMPER philosophies will provide the platform for anyone who wishes to reflect on how to create the kind of life you want to be leading."

**—Cara Marie DiEnno, PhD, Associate Director of the Center for Community Engagement & Service Learning, University of Denver**

"Sarah Plummer Taylor has earned the right, through trial by fire, to be regarded as a rising star among life coaches. Her story about yoga in Iraq and how it saved her life shows how this age-old tradition works and continues into the 21st century. If you think yoga is a crock of hippie hocus-pocus, read about the obstacles Sarah has had to face to understand and express her own capacities. *Choose to Live* could be another title of this book."

**—Rob Schware, PhD, Executive Director of the Give Back Yoga Foundation; President of the Yoga Service Council; www.GiveBackYoga.org**

"Sarah's book takes readers on a thrilling, emotional roller coaster ride framed by principles of her uniquely optimistic and courageous approach to living. This is a must read for those who want to live life to its fullest! Stop whining and start living! That's what Sarah motivates you to do in this amazing book that details her journey in overcoming some of the toughest obstacles you can imagine. This book will inspire you, shock you, challenge you, and charm you."

**—M. J. Clark, Leadership Consultant at Integrated Leadership Systems**

"My sister gave me your book *Just Roll With It!* not too long ago, and I just wanted to tell you how awesome and inspiring it was for me. I'm currently an oncology nurse at the veteran's hospital in Tampa bay and also going to school full time to be an oncology nurse practitioner, so my life is very busy and full of plenty of negative, sad experiences. I love the work I do, but sometimes it's very hard to stay motivated and enjoy little things in life, as I'm constantly surrounded with illness and death. Reading your book truly spoke to me and the things I value within myself and also the things I need to cultivate and work on. The world needs more positive, inspiring people like you! The book spoke on such a holistic level, which is something I pursue in my nursing career. Thank you for the inspiring words."

**—Joyce Hendricks, RN**

"The powerful guide you hold in your hands is written for survivors of trauma by one of the most dynamic, inspiring, caring, and authentic 'thrivors' you'll ever meet. The practical and powerful techniques Sarah Plummer Taylor shares in *Just Roll With It!* have transformed her life and the many lives of those she has touched, coached, and mentored. Her techniques have helped survivors of combat stress, sexual assault, divorce, tragic accidents, loss, and trauma of every shape, size, and color. . . . Sarah is courageous in sharing her own raw story of tragedy, trial, and triumph. But most importantly, in these pages, she takes us by the hand through her SEMPER philosophy and shows us how we can live a life of purpose and meaning, free from the chains of trauma that bind us. Readers who apply and embrace Sarah's SEMPER philosophy will *not* be magically transported back to who they were before their trauma. They *will*, however, become a greater, new, and improved version of themselves, filled with light, freedom, clarity, and purpose to serve and thrive."

**—Larry Broughton, former Special Forces Operator; award-winning entrepreneur and CEO; best-selling author and keynote speaker; founder of broughtonhotels.com and broughtonadvisory.com**

"If you are ready to live a more happy, healthy, and successful life, then read and absorb the strategies in this brilliant book by my friend, Sarah Plummer Taylor."

**—James Malinchak, featured on ABC's hit TV Show** *The Secrete Millionaire*; **co-author of** *Chicken Soup for the College Soul,* **founder of www.BigMoneySpeaker.com**

"Sarah is a strong, honest voice. She has faced intense challenges that could have buried her figuratively and/or literally. But she decided to live and speak with powerful authenticity to inspire and inform others. This book is relevant for veterans, but not just veterans. This book is relevant for human beings as we all, at one point or another, face a challenge that may appear to be insurmountable."

**—Robin Carnes, Trauma-Sensitive Yoga Teacher and Founder of Warriors at Ease; www.WarriorsAtEase.org**

"Sarah's courage will move and inspire you. She's a true warrior. Her enthusiasm is contagious, as is her kindness. She imparts what she's learned from some incredible life experiences with compassion and a genuine desire to help and serve others. Tune in, because Sarah will motivate you to be your absolute best!"

**—Anu Bhagwati, former Marine Corps Captain, Service Women's Action Network founder, and yoga and meditation instructor**

"Heartfelt, clear, applicable lessons. *Just Roll With It!* is a joy to read. Sarah's tone is witty, warm, and honest as she shares some simple principles for improving our own strength and resilience. Intended for those who want real tips on how to make change—to smile, act, and embrace agency without wallowing or whining about how hard things are. The collection of stories made me laugh! It left me thinking. Savvy advice is expressed throughout."

**—Dr. Kate Hendricks Thomas, PhD; USMC Veteran; Assistant Professor of Health Promotion at Charleston Southern University; author of *Brave, Strong, and True: The Modern Warrior's Battle for Balance***

"*Just Roll With It!* is an incredibly inspiring read. With practical tips and suggestions, it's a book that's bound to inspire you to live the best life you've imagined. Sarah's writing is impeccable and her radical authenticity in sharing her personal stories and lessons is as refreshing as it is motivating. If you're feeling stuck or are in need of a shift in your life, Sarah Plummer Taylor and her SEMPER wheel will help you know exactly where to begin."

**—Lisa Theis, yoga instructor, owner of Third Eye Yoga**

"I just want to thank you for sharing your story with the world! Sarah, from the bottom of my heart THANK YOU. Today I finished reading your book. I laughed, I cried, and I healed. I will be sharing this book with others, and I look forward to meeting you one day."

**—Erin Wendlandt, US Marine Corps veteran, yoga teacher**

"I had the pleasure of meeting and spending an entire day with Sarah Plummer Taylor during her Just Roll With It Bootcamp in a time in my life when I needed it most. After reading her book, I feel more inspired than ever knowing that I am on the right path in my life. A happy, healthy, motivated, and full life! Thank you, Sarah, for sharing your story and inspiring me to live in each moment and love my life!!"

**—Kendall Gill, US Coast Guard veteran**

"AMAZING!! A great life message. The more I read your book the more it is key to take your own advice. I am going to send your book to my daughter in Afghanistan as soon as I finish it. She will thrive with the advice. Thank you a million times over!"

**— Jill Willig Chambers, US Army Colonel (ret); founder of This Able Vet**

"Refreshing, inspiring, and fun to read. Sarah Plummer Taylor is one of the most inspiring, authentic, and motivational leaders of our generation. Filled with heartfelt, playful stories, *Just Roll With It!* delivers seven simple, yet extremely powerful SEMPER strategies to help you overcome adversity and thrive personally and professionally. Sarah genuinely walks her talk, naturally connecting with readers and audiences around the world with an energetic, refreshing, and vibrant spirit. *Just Roll With It!* shows you how a happy, healthy lifestyle is really that easy!"

**—Nathalie Osborn, founder of FunEnergyNow.com.**

"Sarah Plummer Taylor's *Just Roll With It!* is an absolute must read! She takes you by the hand and shows you how traits such as faith, sincerity, motivation, and perseverance can lead you beyond your traumas and into a happier and healthier life."

**—Matt Patterson, author of *My Emily***

"All of us go through adversity, and some of us—like Sarah Plummer Taylor—choose to take those lessons and create something truly magical and meaningful. Sarah's 'SEMPER' wheel of principles, grounded in faith, provides readers with a daily inspirational guide to lead truly 'significant' lives. You are truly blessed to read this magnificent book. Let Sarah help you accept yourself for all you are so that you may accomplish all that you are supposed to be."

**—Dr. Danny Brassell, America's Leading Reading Ambassador and founder of The Lazy Readers' Book Club**

"*Just Roll With It!* is a really authentic, accessible, and inspiring introduction to your 'SEMPER' philosophy. I have read many self-help and 'positive psychology' books, and I found yours to be fresh and inclusive. I love the variety of quotes that you have and how you manage to weave Christianity, yoga, and your military training together in a compatible way! Your sincerity is apparent and, I think, key to the success of your book (and any endeavor, ideally)."

**—Sarah Neary, LMSW, RYT**

"Sarah is spot on with everything she describes while being in the USMC. Despite being attacked before she entered the Marines, her warrior spirit got her through her tour of duty. Being cheated from flight school and being told she could not fly did not stop her. She has now reached new heights never before imagined."

**—Frank Soriano, US Marine Corps veteran**

"Sarah's life journey is inspiring and thought provoking. Her philosophy of 'just roll with it' is a transforming message every man, woman, and child will benefit from. As a father of two daughters, Sarah is a person I want my girls to learn from."

**—Jerry Franklin Poe, author of *What I Wish I Knew When I Was in . . . College*, founder of POEtential.com**

"At first, your impression may be that this is just 'another self-help book.' After only a few pages that theory is thrown quicker and further than a live grenade. Inside is the spirit of the Corps, a deep look inside using Marine Corps values, which at the center post is faith. Sarah inspires not by catchy phrases but real-life experiences infused with faith and the Marine Corps ethos as her guiding light. Marines have the EGA emblazoned on their soul. Sarah's shines brightly on every page. A must read for all."

**—Mary Ann Merritt, Women Marines Association, Public Relations Officer**

"A book everyone should read. Sarah's SEMPER strategies really are something that everyone should learn and implement in their life. While I don't have any experience with the military or overly traumatic events, this book was very relatable and a great read. Sarah's message is a message that is for everyone. This book made me laugh, cry, and grow as a person. I truly believe I am a stronger/better person after reading this. I highly recommend you do yourself a favor and get this book for yourself and all of your loved ones!"

**—Peter Taylor**

"*Just Roll With It!* captures your attention from the moment you read it. Sarah's advice helps you change your life for the better, based on her own hardships and real-life combat experiences that allowed her to develop the SEMPER strategies. It's a genuine, heart-felt approach to living every day with your best foot forward, connecting with others around you with positivity and hope, and 'cutting the cords' to put your negative past behind you."

**— Prescott Paulin, International Research Consultant at 300 Below Inc.; US Marine Corps veteran**

"If only more material in today's world could frame adversity into life's biggest learning opportunities the way *Just Roll With It!* does. Battle tested indeed, Sarah has triumphed over personal adversity numerous times and uniquely paints a picture, chapter by chapter, on how the biggest challenges shaped her life in an enlightening, not damaging way. Sarah is a true display of courage, resilience, authenticity, and vulnerability, using her life experience as an opportunity to peel back the layers of perception and become her true self. Sarah's book will inspire, encourage, and shake up the perspective of the reader, leaving them ready to start their journey."

**—Dan Stover, Leadership Consultant at Integrated Leadership Systems**

"This book is a must read for all veterans leaving active duty. As South East Marine for Life, I spent three years preparing Marines for the challenges they would face during their civilian transition. I wish I could have given each of them this book because it will help veterans create a plan that will succeed in any situation life brings. This book focuses on 'the rudder,' a plan to enjoy life and living. Sarah shares her experiences and heartaches as if you were best friends. You will identify personally with most of her journey and learn how to understand your own. Veterans of all services will be glad that they read Semper Sarah's ideas."

**—Jeff Rooks, US Marine Corps veteran**

"Sarah is a lot like me. A military veteran and UVA grad who has learned to roll with the punches. She has found what works and enthusiastically shares her positive ways of life. She gives vivid examples of how her vision works and why. You can feel her passion for life, and helping others improve their lives, dripping off the page. If you want to live a better life and improve the lives around you, this book is for you. Sarah is living her dream life authentically, and she gives back to the world over and over again by sharing her secrets of a good life by being vulnerable about her past, present, and future."

**—Marlene Hall, US Air Force veteran**

"The innovative ideas and approaches in *Just Roll With It!* are the same ones Sarah uses when interacting with today's Veteran generation, ideas which have been the vanguard of VFW Post 1's programs and services. It is only with the fresh interactions such as Sarah's that the needs of today's Veterans be met and that let organizations such as ours tackle those challenges."

**—Michael Mitchel, Commander/Executive Director Veterans of Foreign Wars Post 1, Denver, CO**

# DEDICATION

To Pete, you are my rock.

To Bailey, my three-legged wonder-dog inspiration.

To those who have served past, present, and are yet to in the future.

# CONTENTS

# FOREWORD

I think about *resilient leadership* all the time; it is the focus of my work as a health professional and academic researcher. A pretty phrase, it is almost in vogue right now in corporate circles, but it means little if not imbued with a servant leader's deeper purpose.

Sarah Plummer Taylor understands leadership as more than simply setting the conditions for others to succeed. She leads, teaches, and coaches because she believes in her responsibility to inspire. She shares and advocates to enrich the lives of others out of a sense of mission and from a place of authentic calling.

She writes for the same reason. Utterly without shame or ego, Sarah shares her stories complete with all their real flaws and foibles. Her sincere wish is to share the lessons that anyone can take from her experiences, regardless of the similarity of paths walked.

I met Sarah when we were training to become Marines, which was also the first time I really learned anything about the responsibility members of a team have to lift one another up. Going through introductory level schools was an interesting challenge. Women comprise 4 percent of the Officer Corps, and we are always eyed with suspicion. Our peers constantly measure our abilities to speak intelligently, demonstrate strength, and perform on par physically. The concept of *carrying one's weight* came to matter literally in these early training experiences. We could not fail to perform a task or meet a challenge, because our peers would have to pick up our slack and would suffer for it.

Leading from a platform of strength was important, but you also had to be fearless when speaking or arguing with someone. In an organization like the USMC, if you demonstrate a weak personality, you will not be afforded the opportunity to try again. We not only had to be right, we had to be smart and forceful in the conveyance of ideas.

At my first duty station, I remember meeting my platoon sergeant's young son one afternoon. After meeting me, he turned to his father and stage-whispered in incredulity, "Dad, that's a girl!" The fact was, I was the only platoon commander my Marines had. If I lacked confidence and ability, they would suffer for my incompetence. Failure wasn't an option, especially when we deployed. I had to know what I was doing and demonstrate confidence in my abilities, regardless of how many times the Iraqi Corrections Officers looked at me in shock and asked to speak to the man in charge.

I know both Sarah and I came away from our experiences as leaders of Marines knowing with absolute certainty that leadership is a privilege and requires competence, hard work, and unselfish dedication to the people being served. It is not about ego, money, individual prestige, or ambition. Leading other people requires cooperation and a steadfast willingness to demonstrate a steep learning curve on whatever may be required to accomplish the mission.

I came to believe that at heart, good leaders are both students and teachers.

*We cannot teach people anything, we can only help them discover it within themselves.*

–Galileo

For most of us, personal satisfaction is highest when we feel like we are doing something valuable, when we are living a life of balance that honors our innate spiritual side, and when we are contributing to a larger cause. *Just Roll With It!* is Sarah's service-work offering, and her joyful attempt to reach out and connect with all of us.

Writing is always a risk, one leaders take in hopes of leaving a light on for those wandering. We share our stories and our musings in hopes of making things easier for someone else.

There is purpose to be found in these pages, and I strive to remember the lessons they teach each and every day.

Read this book with an open mind and heart, and give yourself the opportunity to grow.

**—Dr. Kate Hendricks Thomas, author of Brave, Strong, and True: The Modern Warrior's Battle for Balance**
**www.katehendricksthomas.com**

# Chapter 1

## WHY THIS BOOK? WHY NOW?

B ecause it is time.
This book is about resilience and posttraumatic growth, moving beyond trauma, and creating a life we love.

What if we lived in a world where people trusted themselves and others, felt connected, and gave themselves grace and patience during difficult transitions? What if, at their core, people knew they had a choice? What if our *veterans* know they have a choice?

We've all heard the statistic: twenty-two veterans a day are dying by suicide. Well, the stuff that potentially saves veterans from killing themselves is the same stuff that can make us a more compassionate parent, a more forgiving and loving partner, a more effective executive, and a more resilient human being.

Mindful, intentional choice is the act that transforms the energy of any situation and *keeps* us on a path of resilience, as bumpy as that path may be.

Mindful choice requires awareness, awareness of things that are sometimes very painful; but it's only on the other side of awareness that healing takes place.

We hear a lot about posttraumatic *stress*, but let's think about posttraumatic *growth* and the places where we *do* heal. One of the ways people can heal from trauma is through the vehicle of choice. Growth is possible by choosing to change our relationship with trauma by choosing to move through trauma mindfully, versus avoiding it, burying it, or checking out of life, or remaining stuck in our trauma, repeating the story to ourselves over and over again.

In this book, I do want to talk about choices. This may be a hot button topic in the context in which I will address it because some may say that we cannot choose our life, or choose what happens to us after something terrible occurs. Choice is complex. There are people who live in marginalized and oppressed segments of our society who have little choice in matters that may be no big deal to some people. There is even a lot of human behavior that looks like choice, but in reality is a coalescence of all sorts of forces acting upon that individual—like genetic factors, environment, and otherwise—to lead that person to make choices that may be the best thing they can do in that moment. Some research shows, for instance, some people have mental illnesses or other powerful factors that render them incapable of certain choices. Moreover, especially in the context of trauma, there is much guilt, shame, and self-blame involved in situations in which the victim feels they didn't make the "right" choice in a situation in which they didn't really even have one. And it's only at the point that they realize they had no other choice (they didn't have all the intelligence, or the person broke into their house, etc.) and that even if what they did seemed inconsistent with expectations of what they "could've" or "should've" done, the point at which their healing starts is when the person realizes: "No, there really wasn't anything differently I could've done at that time."

Therefore, my intent with what follows on these pages is not to judge or to compound feelings of guilt. Rather, it is to say this: in the situations in which the power to choose is available, this book is designed to help with that. The fact of the matter is, we are all acting at the best capacity that we can, and the choice may or may not always be available. I'm not saying that everything in life is choosable. This book is geared toward empowering us to choose within the moments, within the scope of what's possible, the things that are within our realm of control or our power to change or to choose.

This book's purpose is not to discuss macro-level issues, even though I understand that they are very important. I believe systemic solutions are possible to those larger challenges, but I feel called to speak to the individual, for whom I *do* believe choice is possible in most moments. I assume that if you've picked this book up, then you are one of those people who has the ability to choose, who has power, and who has responsibility. And I believe every one of us has a choice not only every day, but with every single breath.

So, I would like to share a few stories with you about choice. The first story I'd like to share is the one that sort of started it all, and it is about intuition.

It was the summer of 2001. I was in Texas, at Lackland AFB, running up the barracks stairwell with a huge duffle bag on my back, when my left hamstring basically gave way. A moment in time that I'd been training for for years, suddenly stood still. Before knowing the exact details of the culprit of the pain, I knew something had majorly shifted.

I pulled my hamstring on the first day of Air Force Reserve Officer Training Corps (ROTC) field training, then spent five days limping around and muscling through all the events, popping 800mg Motrins like they were Pez, and going through the motions. The pain never subsided though, and I found myself at a crossroads: whether or not I was going to stay at field training and finish with an injury, which I would've been allowed to do, or ask to return the next year when I was fully healthy.

So less than a week into field training, when the pain became too much to bear, I had to call my parents (one of whom is a retired Air Force Colonel) with the bad news. I was lectured and told if I came home early, I would be failing to keep a commitment I had made. After much debate, to include strong consideration of "sucking it up," given how directly it negatively impacted my training, I was told that I probably did need to come home. So I did.

I was devastated because when I hurt my leg at Air Force Field Training, it was kind of a shock to my main existence and source of identity in life, which was to succeed at my military training. I felt like I was letting everyone down. But once I got home and had time to process what had happened, I realized I could see this obstacle as either something that was going to stop me *or* I could see it as an opportunity.

Because honestly, the injury was actually a wake-up call. It made me pause, reassess, and reflect. I didn't want to be a victim to my injured leg. I saw it as an opening because deep down, intuitively, I knew the Air Force was not for me.

This was my first memorable experience with the "mind-body connection"—not that I would have framed it that way at the time. My body was trying to get my attention in a way that my mind couldn't reach me because I'd out-reasoned myself into staying in the Air Force. My hamstring snap was a wake-up call, one I believe I received both from God and from my internal self saying, *"This is not where you're supposed to be."*

A few weeks later, I returned to college and I met with both the Marine Corps commanding officer and the Air Force commanding officer of the respective ROTC units, and I declared my intent to switch services.

It was not an easy thing to do, emotionally or logistically, but it was *possible* because I hadn't completed Air Force Field Training; there was a loophole in the contract that allowed me to switch my commitments. However, this intent to switch set off a string of cautionary lectures from my Air Force leadership as well as letters and phone calls from my father saying he would never approve of this decision and that I was ruining my life. This is part of one of his letters to me, his then twenty-year-old daughter, one week before 9/11. He said:

> The USMC is about ground attack. You will never lead troops in a ground attack (thank God) and that will limit you whether you believe it or not. I've been around all the services. I take the Air Force hands down, and I want only the best for you. I will never say I agree with you becoming a Marine. I KNOW the Air Force is a better, more rewarding life. You can believe all you want that you can make it in the macho world of the Marines, that you can make them accept you . . . You will never be a man, you will never be as mean, nasty, tough, strong, etc. The Marines are built on that concept for a reason. It does not matter what they say to be politically correct. They have to believe they are meaner, nastier, and tougher than the enemy bastard whose throat they have to slit on a dark night. We need people like that. Maybe you can do that, maybe you want to do that, but no high-school dropout, weighing 210 pounds with an IQ of 90 is ever going to believe that. I'm sorry if this sounds cruel or perhaps wrong to you, but I know it is true. Should

you have the right to prove yourself? Yes. Will you? I doubt it. PFTs are not Iwo Jima's beach where you have a 60lb pack on your back, the water is chest high, the surf is pounding in your face, bullets are whistling around your head, mortars are blowing your unit into hamburger, and you have to turn and say "follow me." I know you want to fly and all this death and destruction is far less personal, unless of course you are shot down and taken prisoner (if you survive the crash). Hopefully you will never have to fight a war, but you are joining (either AF or USMC) to do that if called upon. It's about believing you are right so much that you are willing to do whatever is necessary to win. To kill someone else face-to-face or with a bomb. Decide you can do it. Decide you convince others to do it. About flying. I know from first-hand experience that just wanting to be a pilot isn't enough. I was smart, I was tough, I had more desire than most, but I didn't have enough of whatever to make it. I wasn't a bad person or a failure because of it, but I had to find a different job. So don't ignore this. I'm not trying to jinx you, but you are not being fair to yourself if you don't think about the options. . . . Yes, you will always be my daughter and I will always love you. I will accept your decision, but I will never tell you that the Marines are better for you than the Air Force. It's more than the fact that I was in the Air Force too. I have no doubt the Air Force will be everything you are seeking in the military, and more. . . . You will have something of an uphill fight in any service because you are a woman. Don't kid yourself. It isn't right but it is true. You will be a minority. People will respect you for your intelligence more in the Air Force. . . . I hope this isn't too late. I want you to stay in the Air Force.

I love you. Dad

But deep down, in my gut, in my heart, I knew the Marines was where I was supposed to be. I felt *called* to be a Marine.

Explaining that to your Air Force father who you love and admire is a difficult task.

23

I didn't just rely on myself during that transition from Air Force to Marine Corps ROTC, though, as strong as I thought I was at twenty years old. I chose to also rely on the support of my closest friends, who heard me belabor the details of the switch over and over again and gave me good advice, who helped me train and prepare to become a Marine, and helped me keep things light when the whole situation felt quite heavy at times. Also, my mentors at school were incredibly helpful, to include the Marine Officer Instructor, a Major in the Marines, and the Assistant MOI, a Gunnery Sergeant, who believed in me, encouraged me, and trained me to succeed during the transition and beyond. I was never left to do the work alone.

Here's the universal point: we've all been in a situation where we thought we might disappoint someone we love because of the choices we make about our particular path. Yet, to continue to live in a way that is out of alignment with who we are at our very core, can destroy us.

Connection, camaraderie, and community are vital, and every success story includes support from other people. All of my healthy transitions certainly involve the love and support of countless others.

Yet, I believe we must also pay attention to our support from within, from our bodies. Not a visual of a youthful, fit, svelte body, but a supportive body that is an ally for action and balance, that is a resource of wisdom for us.

Although the power of intuition is something that's hard to describe with *words*, it's easy to *feel* within ourselves. We all know this when we say things like: "I just felt it in my gut" or "I knew it in my heart." Intuition requires awareness, that sometimes painful awareness, and we can choose to ignore our intuitions or we can choose to act on them.

How do we cultivate the habit of listening to our intuitive selves though? How do we listen to that intuition that lives in our hearts and our guts? We practice tuning in (in a variety of ways I'll share later), or we can try this: When you are about to make a decision, or potentially mistreat yourself or your body, pause, and ask yourself, "Is this how I would treat a good friend?" Our answer will come. And this is one basic way to begin practicing awareness.

Our bodies are not machines. "Do you not know that your bodies are temples of the Holy Spirit, who is in you, whom you have received from God? You are not your own" (1 Corinthians 6:19). Let's celebrate that we have a trusted friend (our bodies) to accompany us on our journey. Even when it supposedly "breaks," we can attempt to actually celebrate the wisdom within our bodies, injuries and all, and be grateful for the messages that we receive from it, and its ability to be our greatest ally, because it is the house of our intuition. Our bodies want to faithfully support us. Our bodies help us find power *within* ourselves, not *over* ourselves.

Our bodies empower us to choose.

The second story I'd like to share with you in this introduction of the book is about agency, the power of our own choices. (Warning: this story includes some detail about sexual assault.)

A second formative choice I made happened a couple years later in 2003. I was a 2nd Lieutenant in the United States Marine Corps (so the switch happened in case you were wondering), and in first week of The Basic School (TBS), I was doing my best to drink from the proverbial firehouse and absorb all the information we heard during orientation week.

One of the briefs we received was from the Judge Advocate General (the JAG). With sarcasm and disdain, she warned a roomful of new officers about one of the most common "legal issues" we'd face while there: that we were likely going to rape one another at some point in our six-month training program. And it hit me, *What if the guy who raped me comes here and does that to someone else? I will never be able to live with myself.*

And I had a choice.

I *had* been raped, four months before, by a peer. And as the JAG told one particular story about a lieutenant raping another lieutenant there at The Basic School that sounded eerily similar to mine, I turned my head to the right, and, in a room of more than two hundred lieutenants, locked eyes with my friend who I had called right after the assault. From across the room she mouthed, "You have to tell."

I mouthed back, "I know."

The day after I was raped, I went to my Marine Officer Instructor (MOI), the major who served as the leader of the Marine Corps-bound students within the Navy ROTC Battalion, and told him I didn't want to be a Marine anymore. I told him that I'd seen some things recently that made me believe I couldn't, shouldn't, and no longer wanted to be associated with the Marines. I intended on telling my MOI that day that I had been raped. I didn't though, and I'll share more about that story later in the book.

But I know why victims do not want to tell, because before *it* happens to you, you never think that it *could* happen to you, a strong, self-reliant person like you. But it did.

I sucked it up though. I swallowed it and let it fester inside of me.

Then four months later, I reported to Quantico Marine Corps Base as a 2nd Lieutenant. I completed Introductory Flight School (IFS), and then awaited my start of The Basic School, which is where this particular story began. That one day during orientation week of TBS, I sat in one of our classrooms and listened to the JAG describe other incidents of rape and sexual assault that had occurred between Marines at the training command. As I said, she was flippant, sarcastic, and insincerely warned us about being careful not to get raped by each other.

So I knew the military was notorious for mishandling rape cases.

Despite all of that, I felt like it was my duty to report it to possibly protect any potential future victims. I was terrified the legal proceedings would take exactly the route that they did—isolation, fear, repeated questioning that left me feeling like the perpetrator, a disruption of my training cycle, and irrevocable damage to many of my personal relationships.

Although awful that it happened in the first place, and somehow even more awful going through the reporting process, choosing to report the rape gave me agency.

Agency is that feeling of having a grip on your life, having a sense of influence or the feeling of being in charge of your own life. Yes, even in the midst of chaos.

It is not something I would have chosen, of course—to have been raped—but given the option of staying in a black hole within myself or doing something that I felt could potentially protect a future victim, and something that gave me a sense of power of standing up for myself, reporting was one of the best choices I ever made. As hard as it was and as damaging as it was to my personal and professional life in some ways, it was a choice that gave me power.

This is the universal point of this story: we all have these moments where we can choose to do the "hard" thing—often the "right" thing—*or* choose to keep our intuition, our character, or even our conviction to speak up on behalf of someone else buried.

Speaking up puts this dark thing into the light.

Even though it was around something negative, it made me focus, it gave me purpose, and it made me connect to resources. As vulnerable as I already felt, it made me be more vulnerable in a way that guided me toward a deeper connection with others. I formed deep friendships with those few who knew what I was going through. I sought professional counseling, I confided in family, and I began a journey of self-healing, introspection, and reflection that continues to this day. It fueled my ability to continue to sustainably serve even after I left the service.

My assailant, a peer, someone I knew, came into my home and attacked me.

He made a choice. Most of us have been hurt by something or someone who made a really bad choice.

Most of us have hurt ourselves at times too.

Yet we still have agency; we still have power to choose again in the future.

The third story I'd like to share with you is about self-awareness and our ability to observe and notice without judgment. I consider it one of the most important choices I've made in my life.

I was twenty-six years old. I was on a single bed, alone, in my can—my room—in Iraq.

It would be a lie to say I "awoke in bed" in these morning moments, because I went days at a time without actually sleeping. I had racing thoughts about the harassment I dealt with on a daily basis during that deployment. I had nightmares about the threats being made against me. I had nightmares about having been raped by one of my friends, a fellow service member, a few years before. I had nightmares about having lost my marriage at twenty-two. And the physical pain I was in (from scoliosis, arthritis, herniated discs, chronic migraines, digestive problems, and various symptoms from a variety of nearly a dozen traumatic brain injuries) kept me in a constant state of wincing. I was in my 20s, looked like I was in my 30s, and felt like I was in my 80s.

As I lay in bed, my eyes opened. The first thing I saw was my pistol. Just a simple, black, standard Marine Corps issue M9 pistol. It was hanging on my bedpost in the brown leather holster that my ex-boyfriend gave me. (Because those are the gifts you give a loved one when you're in the Marines).

And I saw my $20 beige yoga mat—almost the same color of the sand I was always surrounded by—rolled up at the foot of my bed between it and my wall locker.

My room was big enough for a wall locker, a single bed, and a yoga mat to be rolled out on the floor next to it.

I blinked. It was excruciating to exist. And I thought to myself it'd just be easier if I just weren't here. And I had a choice: the pistol or the yoga mat. It was life or death. I could keep inhaling, I could inspire, or I could exhale for the last time; I could expire.

Here's the universal point: we all have these moments where we have to make big choices, where we find ourselves in battle zones feeling completely alone. And when we feel that we are separate, that we have no purpose, that we have no power, we end up choosing death literally or symbolically. We give up. We quit. But the biggest lie we believe is that we are alone. We are never alone. And what if we choose life?

Instead of holding our breath, holding back, holding it all in, or waiting, what if we got on our "yoga mat" and started to breathe? What if our inhales and exhales weren't things we took for granted but which we used to direct our very essence, our focus, our purpose, our intuition, our intention, attention, and connection?

Inhale. Exhale.

Inspire. Expire.

I had an epiphany then that has stuck with me since: my breath was mine; it was the one thing no one could touch. At a time when I felt like every single aspect of my life had someone else's hands on it, they couldn't touch my breath.

The reality is everyone has had a difficult decision to make. Maybe mine was life or death. Potentially, your big decisions have been too! We have the yoga mat choice we can make, or the pistol choice we can make. Like staying on the couch for another hour of TV or getting up to go for a walk or a jog. The pistol or the mat? Like having the same argument with our partners over and over again, or choosing to give counseling a try. The pistol or the mat? Like devouring a pint of ice cream at midnight straight from the carton, standing there with the freezer door open when you are exhausted and not thinking straight, versus having a healthy dinner and then actually going to bed when you're tired. The pistol or the yoga mat? We always have a choice.

The awareness of my own mind-body connection via yoga gave me a sense of power and increased sensitivity. I was able to *sense* what was actually happening within me and respond (versus react) . . . one breath at a time. So my breath gave me choice.

The root of inspire, aspire, and expire is *spirare* from the Latin word meaning to breathe. As we try to inspire others, we fill them with fire, and fire requires oxygen, or breath. As we aspire to do anything, we must breathe life into it. And when we choose to die, we exhale our last breath.

Breathwork refers to many forms of conscious alteration of breathing, such as connecting the inhale and exhale or energetically charging and discharging, when used within psychotherapy, yoga, meditation, or other healing contexts. Teaching and practicing breathwork is a key component of my private health counseling practice not only because I've experienced the benefits first hand but also because research like a Harvard Medical School study from 2013 showed that simply knowing breath-management techniques and having a better understanding and awareness of stress can help build resilience.

The term *meditation* also refers to a broad variety of practices (much like the term *sports*) that includes techniques designed to promote relaxation, build internal energy or life force, guide prayer and focus, and develop compassion, love, and patience.

Yoga is used to direct and enhance the body's energy and aid in the release of old emotions. In a literal sense, yoga is the union of breath and movement to build well-being. Breathwork, meditation, and yoga are the three main components of "mindfulness practices" that I've utilized for myself and for others with whom I work in my health counseling practice, in consulting for corporations or veterans' groups, and on the wellness and resilience retreats I lead. Research shows that mindfulness practices light up the compassion center of our brains and helps us form new neural pathways, whether it's been ravaged by trauma and stress or normal confusion and daily distractions. Day in, day out, we live with stress, and that's actually okay. We *do* require stress to survive.

What matters is how stress affects our nervous system and how we process it emotionally based on how we perceive its impact. So mind-set is pretty important! We'll never eliminate stress completely; that is not the aim. The aim is to improve our relationship with feelings of stress, anxiety, and depression, ultimately learning to tolerate distress. Maybe this is the other side of the coin for most of us who are goal oriented and want to eliminate symptoms. But I've found that focusing solely on eliminating symptoms can get us either stuck in them or magnify them. Breathwork is one major tool that helps us smooth the edges of the spikes and dips.

So, the aim is to be resilient in the face of stress. The aim is to be dynamic and responsive, not stagnant and reactive. We must surf the waves, not strive to make them stop. And we need to know how to do that.

Every day, twenty-two veterans kill themselves. Every day, twenty-two veterans feel separate, alone, misunderstood, and hardened to the world. And these mindfulness practices can help veterans stop ending their own lives. These tools are not nice to haves; they are lifesavers!

Maybe veterans have more experience with a particular type of pain and trauma than the average American, but we *all* have pain and trauma; we all have battle zones like divorce, illness, loss of a loved one, financial hardship, chronic business, and times when we feel like we have control over nothing.

Pain is a teacher; we have a choice to respond or react to our teaching. We have the power to choose the life we want. Recognizing that power can be scary at first, but if we can cultivate curiosity and awareness in our own choices, we're moving in the right direction. How can pain be a teacher and not an enemy?

We need to think of stress, resilience, and posttraumatic growth less as treatment and more as opportunities for training. Because let's be serious, the veteran mind-set is not one that responds well to victimization or pathologizing of their problems. We need to be more proactive. We need to help soldiers, sailors, airmen, and Marines up-armor ahead of time with tools they can take with them anywhere in any situation. All

Post-Traumatic Stress (PTS) does *not* come just from combat. It comes from those other battlefields too. Even for those in treatment settings, if we can design it to be more like training so we can destigmatize health practices to be presented as mindfulness and resiliency building toolsets that "bulletproof" our brains, we'll be speaking the language of resiliency, of awareness, of agency, of connection, and ultimately of CHOICE.

What if my peer group and I had been taught to respect the waves of anxiety, depression, and stress that surely come as a survivor of chaos, sexual trauma, or combat just as a surfer is taught to respect the strong waves of the ocean? To revere them, train for them, and honor their wisdom? What if I had understood things that way? What if our warriors today can cultivate that understanding? To be able to respect and honor our minds and bodies instead of feeling betrayed by them is a game changer that mindfulness fuels.

Intuition, agency, connection, and awareness are all choices. They don't just happen. We can choose to act, even little bits at a time, and we can choose to connect, one breath at a time.

I'd like to offer you a way to connect now, with some simple and powerful breathwork. This is just one type of breathwork I frequently use with my clients and students, as well as in my daily practices, and it is called "square breath." It is known to calm our nervous system and get us "grounded" and connected to our bodies. It can sometime produce a feeling of "balance," as well.

So, who knew there were so many ways to breathe? This is just one. Here we go.

Sit somewhere comfortable, either on the ground or in a chair. If in a chair, if possible, place both feet flat on the floor and sit up straight, but not rigid. To start, close your mouth gently and keep your jaw relaxed while you begin to inhale and exhale just through your nose. Do that a few times, then begin square breath: inhale as you count to 4, then pause and hold your breath in (but stay relaxed in the face, jaw, and shoulders in particular!) for a count of 4, then exhale to a count of 4, and then pause and hold the breath out for a count of 4. So it's inhale for 4, hold the breath in for 4, exhale for 4, hold the breath out for 4. Start by practicing five rounds of that. Increase this gradually as you develop your breathing practice. Then give yourself a minute to two to sit quietly afterward, simply breathing in whatever way feels comfortable.

Increasing our awareness of our mind-body connection can be *so* helpful because we can seriously outthink ourselves in our heads! But the body knows better. And the body is the avenue for accessing our spirit. So, instead of working to tame the body, master it, and lord over it, we should respect it for the messenger that it is. Because if we're willing to connect to it, we, as trauma survivors, just might have a chance . . . heck, better than a chance, we can actually thrive!

And so this is what I would say to veterans seeking posttraumatic growth: choice is powerful. We don't have to choose life or death; we can choose to honor the rising *and* the falling of the waves. It's like saying, "Should I inhale or exhale?" We must do both. Just breathe. Breathwork is action. Breath is the instigator of change. Breath transforms, empowers, and renews. Breath is our very life force. Breath has the power to create, to destroy, and to transform. Breath unites. Your exhale is my inhale. Breath is an avenue to spirit. Breath makes space for choice.

Even when all else is raging around us, swirling in our respective battle zones, the one thing we can always *choose* is our breath. It changes our brains, our bodies, and our hearts. It's always ours. It's on the house— it's free! No one can ever touch it. It's the one thing we all do all the time whether we want to or not. It unites us to our strongest self and helps us connect to others.

Our lives begin and end with breath, and in the space in between, intentional breath helps us make intentional choices.

I know I've caught myself saying these things, and perhaps you have too, when someone has encouraged you to try something new: "I'm too busy." "I'm too tired." "Money is tight." "I don't know how to do that." "I'm too old." "That sounds weird." But what if we believed we were *really* worth it? What if we were willing to make the choice to put ourselves where we really—REALLY—wanted to be? Where we claim we want to be? Being who we are meant to be? With the people we are meant to be with? Doing the work we are meant to do? Living the adventures we are meant to live? And believing, wholeheartedly, in the things we are burning to believe in? Feeling nourished on a mind, body, and spirit level where all our internal systems worked in concert with one another instead of seemingly against one another? What if, through less pushing and pulling, we found more ease, a sense of peace, or a feeling of well-being? What if?

Because there's still CHOICE woven into all chaos, and it requires accountability to ourselves. Accountability doesn't equal blame or fault. Choice actually means a halting of blame shifting. Choice means accepting the tough stuff, and the baggage too, and realizing it really does make us stronger. Because choice is powerful, even small choices.

A small shift I found very helpful was to start to think more about "adding in" some "good" things in order to "crowd out" the "bad" things, and focusing less on feeling like I had to take bad things out of my life. I began to think more about things that nourished me and fed me on all levels, and as I added in more and more of those things, they crowded out the bad stuff. (By the way, this works with food *and* relationships). In the military, we were taught to reinforce success not failure. So we should keep reinforcing the things that *work*, one little bit at a time, and trust that the compound effect of those small choices end up making big differences in the long run.

Small choices work because if we choose it, we can change it! Once we start to *own* our choices, we can MAKE our choices, but it's hard to make our choices when we are either stuck in our stuff or completely tuned out, right? We basically have two major coping mechanisms to deal with pain, stress, and anxiety: we either cognitively fuse to our thoughts and get stuck in them as we ruminate on our problems and cannot see or feel anything else or engage with anyone else . . . ooooor, we deny, tune out, and ignore. We implement experiential avoidance via lots of creative approaches like overworking and feeding the chronic business beast, excessively working out, or using drugs or alcohol. But man if it doesn't all come back around like a boomerang and smack us in the back of the head! Because our problems never go away by ignoring them. So we've got to be PRESENT. Sometimes being present hurts and sucks and we don't want to feel that way, but it's part of the process. The process starts by choosing to do things that are seemingly simple.

I'll give you some specifics. The last few years, I've been doing some things that I previously thought were silly, or didn't imagine to be that impactful, that I now wish I had learned to do many years ago. I have now seen them make an impact on my ability to become healthier and healthier after trauma. I'll give you some examples: consciously breathing on a daily basis; seeing prayer as a practice, not as an obligation; practicing yoga almost every day; making quality sleep a real priority; implementing simple self-care practices that are cheap and not time consuming like body brushing, tongue scraping, and proper skin care; eating less processed food and adding in nutrient-dense foods; getting massages twice a month; bartering with other healers so I can try things like acupuncture and chakra healing; and moving every day (not exercise but daily *movement*)—giving myself permission, for instance, to take a little walk if I don't have time for a long run. When we consider that trauma lives in the body, we need to move our bodies in order to move through trauma.

Also, I make big, scary choices like adjusting relationships by letting go of ones I've had for a long time but no longer serve me or the other person, creating better boundaries with family, starting a business, writing a book, testifying to Congress, traveling alone, or playing new sports.

The good news is that you can do these things too. I saw others doing similar things and began to emulate them. I moved to a new city and joined an Australian Rules football team to meet new people. Who even knows what Aussie Rules are? As kids, we have teachers and coaches, or in the military we have commanding officers, and then as adults or when we get out of the military, we often forget their importance, but we can still have people like that in our lives!

Every success story includes others. Don't be afraid to ask for help.

Start with one of these things. Find a fellowship group at your church, get a mentor or coach, connect with Team Red, White, and Blue or Warriors at Ease, start moving every day, try yoga, drop your soda habit, or start with three minutes of breathwork in the morning if you don't have twenty. You don't have to do it ALL, all today. *Choose to start.*

Back to the story. So, although I began sporadically practicing yoga in the early 2000s in college to deal with overtraining injuries from soccer and ROTC, it was nothing more than creative cross-training to me until I was in the midst of my second deployment in Iraq. Honestly, I'd barely done yoga before I went to Iraq. I didn't even really like it. I was the person who often left in the middle of class or walked out during *savasana* (final resting pose), but I'd heard it was good for you. I had a Marine who was bold enough to keep telling me, "Ma'am, you need this," and he gave me his yoga DVD. So I was willing to take a risk and give it a try again.

Then in Iraq, without even consciously processing the higher transformation that was taking place within me, when I was emotionally distraught, yoga gave me clarity. The simple, basic union of breath and movement made space for the two most important things in my life—my choice and my soul.

Somehow, in a body experiencing very physical effects of depression, and other multiple severe physical injuries, when I practiced yoga, I had less pain. Somehow, in a world that felt like 24/7 chaos, like a battle zone at all times, the mat gave me an anchor point with which to align.

Thank God for that 3' x 6' floor space because it was where I could simply breathe without suffocating. I would roll off my bed and onto my yoga mat and things would change. I would align. I could breathe. If I was lucky, things would release. I would stretch, and then I would breathe, and run and feel free.

Stretch.

Breathe.

Move.

Stretch.

Breathe. Move . . . Breathe.

Connect.

If I was lucky, I *would* connect . . . first to something beyond myself, to God, then to those around me; it meant I was alive. I would repeat to myself, "I'm breathing. I'm alive. I'm breathing. I'm alive." It was that simple for me at that point in my life. To breathe meant to be alive and to be alive meant to believe.

And if I was alive, I *was* connecting spiritually and physically, which then allowed me to stay alive and to connect with those around me, for I certainly was not the only one going through what I was going through. I was not the first or last lost soul who found herself in a battle zone. When I realized that—that my lack of "specialness" was actually a blessing in this case and that my baggage wasn't a burden, but touchstones for growth—the accessibility to healing became greater, deeper, and more diverse.

Yoga and faith bridged the gap and paved a path to long-term healing for me, and I've seen it do it for others. A key component to allowing these mindfulness practices to be healing, and to generate health not just generate more stress and frustration, is to meet yourself where you are instead of judging yourself. Remember, your body is a good friend; ask it what it needs. "Meeting yourself where you are" is a dance between complacency and perfectionism, coupled with trusting that you are stronger than you think you are. It's not even about finding a perfect balance; it's about being comfortable with the rhythm of your authentic ebb and flow, your surges and draw downs, learning what your true center is, where you can align with it and bounce back to it after a stressful or challenging time. Learning to find your intelligent edge that fosters growth, versus pushing yourself to further injury, can take a lifetime to master.

Yes, I've been through some tough times, and so have you. So let's also celebrate the small wins; the daily activities that we can do better because of choice based on intuition, agency, and breath; the more compassionate courses we take with ourselves and others; the activities we choose; the food we choose; the decisions we make; and the paths we walk.

Yes, my faith and yoga saved me, but it was the breath that softened me. The breath gave me the tangible thing to anchor to. Breath was a gateway to believing in my own power again, the power to choose my path, the power to heal, and the power to connect. Breath was a vehicle for choice based on mind-body awareness.

Choose one thing you can do. I chose the mat. What's your mat? Where do you heal?

Because as you heal, you create space for others to heal. As you succeed, you give permission for others to succeed. Never stop trying to bring more light, love, and health into your life and into this world. You are worth it. You are only one choice away from a new beginning. Choose to live!

So, again, I ask, Why this book? Why now?

Because we need more faith, connection, and self-care in our lives, we need deeper and bigger breaths, and because we need to believe in the power of our own intuition, agency, and awareness. We need to know who we are, and then actually act like it! We need to embrace humility and humor more than pretense and perfection. We need more love, friendship, and compassion. We need to reflect without ruminating, and then move on. That is what it means to *Just Roll With It*.

So let's get rollin'!

# Chapter 2

# ROLLING WITH WHAT? WHAT IS SEMPER?

First things first—a warning: This book is imperfect. So am I. So are you. And we're in this thing called *life* together.

I am sometimes a teacher; I am always a student.

Now, here we go!

> *"Everything is changing all the time, and we keep wanting to pin it down, to fix it. So whenever you come up with a solid conclusion, let the rug be pulled out. You can pull out your own rug, and you can also let life pull it out for you. . . . One way to pull out your own rug is by just letting go, lightening up, being more gentle, and not making such a big deal."*
> —Pema Chödrön, *Start Where You Are*

Right on, Pema! We all can take life too seriously sometimes, can't we?

We may work in earnest to "self-develop," then pile to-do's upon ourselves, incessantly compare ourselves to others, compete with everyone in our professional and personal lives, doubt our self-worth because of some trauma or stacked-up stress we have experienced, and round out the day with lots of self-defeating monologues. None of that behavior creates happiness, health, or success.

So, hit the pause button for a hot second. Give yourself a break. All that junk is still going to be there waiting for you if you want to pick it back up at the end of this book. I invite you to use the time in which you read this book like a little sacred space for yourself to say, "The stuff is there, but right now, I'm here. I'm present. I get to take a li'l break."

Picture me, smiling and shouting at you in an *Anchorman* Ron Burgundy voice—and with nothing but love and respect for you in my heart—"Hey, everybody! I have a very important announcement to make . . ."

"Cannonball!"

If you didn't quite get that comedic reference, please watch that movie. You simply must. Okay, so maybe I wouldn't shout "cannonball" at you, but what I might shout is, "Hey, listen up. Your life is at stake!" Those habitual negative thoughts are robbing you of the significant, fulfilling life you crave. They prevent you from being your true and courageously authentic self, empathizing with others, offering self-compassion, and connecting in meaningful ways to form relationships that last. Granted, those thoughts have likely formed deep grooves in your mind from years of conditioning. Habits are hard to break because those neural pathways make imprints on us in a very physical sense, down to the cellular level, and in an intensely real way on our very hearts and souls. The repatterning is the great and messy work of life we get to do together though!

Negative thoughts are the building blocks of the walls we put between others and ourselves. We could be the most capable, intelligent, and beautiful people in the world. Friends, family, and strangers could admire us and be inspired by us, yet if we don't believe we are worthy, then our greatness will be hidden to some degree, unable to get out from underneath the "bushel" and shine its light on the world. Each moment that we doubt our value, every self-defeating thought we allow to dominate our internal monologues, and every ridiculous comparison of our beginning to someone else's end becomes a precious gift of life discarded. Don't you dare waste your talents, your breath, or your life!

Is there a proverbial hamster wheel of negativity or simple, yet insidious, doubt that often runs nonstop through your mind? Do you hear things such as: "I should've run faster on my jog tonight." "I know she said she liked my yoga class, but she was probably just trying to be nice. I'm not that good of a teacher. I should've played different music or taught a different sequence." "I'm not really a good mother because my child isn't doing well in school. I should have smarter kids." "I shouldn't still be angry about that situation, but I am." "She's more successful than I am; I'll never achieve that. I wasn't good enough for that position anyway. I shouldn't do this work." "I should've outplayed that guy on the field." "If I had just said what I really thought at that meeting, the boss would've picked me for the next big project. I should've spoken up."

Stop "should'ing" all over yourself! I encourage you to change things up. Like any desired change, though, it requires rerouting. We need to touch base with our roots and move forward from a strong foundation and aligned core. That's what I hope to help you uncover within yourself in the course of this book. Now, I can't do your push-ups for you, but I'm here to offer some stories, encouragement, and advice along the way. By no means am I asserting that everything in this book should work for you, or work for all people in all situations. Pick a few things that really resonate for you, and start there.

*"Teachers open the door, but you must enter by yourself."*
—Chinese Proverb

I'm happy to open the door, but you gotta walk through it yourself. Part of walking through that door is an element of letting go what is behind you so you can fit through the door. So, as we get going, I'd encourage you to consider even slightly embracing the mere willingness to "let go." Because, let's be honest, sometimes we like clinging to our crap. It's familiar. We know it. But man that stuff can get heavy.

Instead of beating yourself up over your mistakes or imperfections, or trying to hold on to everything in a controlling way—then feeling completely deflated when things don't work out to your liking—let go of those thoughts and just roll with it. When you try to hold on tightly to everything, life is like a bar of soap that slips out of your hands and the achievement you are driving for only slips further and further away.

*"Know that there's room for everyone to be passionate, creative and successful. In fact, there's more than room for everyone; there's a need for everyone."*
—Marianne Williamson

To "just roll with it" is less flippant than it sounds. To "just roll with it" is about *choice*. It's about embracing your own agency. You get to write the story of your life.

You choose your thoughts; your thoughts do not choose you. I know that sounds simple, but it is not necessarily easy. (Remember, *choice is complex*.) Where we can start, though, is realizing that life is never static; we must go with the flow, roll with it, and let go a little, or else we inevitably get stuck where we are. What was the case yesterday may not be the situation today. Change *is* constant; we all know that, but can we *accept* it? Can we observe—then accept—changes within ourselves and others with nonjudgment?

We must allow people to have their moments and their time to process things, just as we should allow it for ourselves. In that spirit, I want to emphasize that I do believe in the value of taking time to digest what has happened to you; rather, just that we don't stay in that space indefinitely. Think of it like doing an After Action Report (AAR) in the military. AARs serve as a standardized feedback and growth cycle for military operations that is just as applicable to our day-to-day lives. *Do an AAR for your life!* Reflection is valuable, but too much time spent there renders you "stuck." Reflect, then move forward. We need literal and metaphorical space to digest our experiences and make adjustments, which empower us to find and follow our purpose.

I have a purpose. My mission is to help you find yours as well. That may sound like a lofty endeavor. The truth is that it's raw and real, gritty and tough going; it's downright terrifying at times to put myself out there in the way I feel God has called me to do. As Nikos Kazantzakis said, though, "True teachers are those who use themselves as bridges over which they invite their students to cross; then, having facilitated their crossing, joyfully collapse, encouraging them to create their own." I am called to help you build your bridges.

I'm also still learning. Remember the warning at the beginning of this chapter? I am imperfect for sure! I'm learning how to invite more trust, compassion, patience, grace, and ease into this process. That's good news actually because it means this stuff can be learned and practiced. It's all a matter of rehearsal in a way, like practicing a sport, maintaining daily prayer and meditation, journaling, or sticking with your yoga practice.

Forming new pathways within ourselves and for ourselves is a *practice*. Which means—thank goodness—we get to mess up along the way!

Look, I think I should probably be dead after the variety of things I've been through, but I'm not and it's because I believe wholeheartedly that I need to authentically and imperfectly share this message of hope, happiness, and health with you. I've been struck by lightning, hit by a car, broken nearly every major bone in my body (and a bunch of little ones), suffered from more than a dozen concussions (from sports, accidents, and during my time in the military), walked away from a devastating car crash that left my car totaled, and was raped by a fellow Marine and spent years battling depression. Although I am significantly healthier now than I have ever been before, I also still cope with the reverberations of Post-Traumatic Stress Disorder and Traumatic Brain Injuries to this day. I take comfort in knowing that not only have I been able to create a life I truly love, I have also been able to transform my crises into opportunities to help others, have a positive impact, share love, and otherwise inspire those in need. Knowing that I've done that for even one person lifts my spirits because then I know I have served my life's purpose.

What are you going to do with *your* one wild and precious life? Are you going to be laden with self-defeating thoughts or stuck in a rut after something did not go your way? Or if you experienced a trauma, tragedy, or difficult life event will you be bitter forever and allow it to cripple your dreams? I hope not! But if you are stuck, I'm here to help.

This is not a clinical therapy book to make you hash through your past, relive dark memories, and from that, supposedly, "figure it out." Isn't that the typical model? And how have you felt after doing those sorts of mental exercises? You might find temporary relief, and I do believe there is value in types of therapies that also bring you back to the present instead of keeping you in the past. This book is about encouraging you to *move forward*. It is a guide for explaining to you how to be present in the now, a now that is fluid, always evolving, always moving, vulnerable, real, stressful and beautiful, and everything in between all at the same time. Healing doesn't mean achieving "perfection" or "fixing" yourself. Healing is a process and a practice. Cultivating the capacity to *mindfully* let go of the past is a key element of that. We can do so by becoming aware of it, then allowing ourselves to *feel* what we do about it, then we bring

43

it into the light by sharing with a trusted someone. That consciousness and process of feeling, naming, and owning the past are the first steps toward potentially then letting a little bit of it go, moving forward, and being present in our day-to-day lives.

Feel it. Name it. Own it. Release it.

*"Trying to make what is temporary last only causes distress. Yes, change upsets the illusion of psychological security. You can either agonize over this and fight it fruitlessly, or you can choose to pierce through the illusion to the truth. When you start coming from a place of acceptance rather than the standard, chronic state of resistant, nonacceptance, your experience of life cannot be stopped from totally changing for the better. Happiness is a function of acceptance."*

—Steve Ross, *Happy Yoga*

Do not mistake acceptance as complacency. Complacency is a defeated contentment with mediocrity, a giving up on your dreams and stopping where you are, a living with something you don't really want. Complacency is a lack of inspiration, and we die inside when we are not living inspired. We can combat complacency's energy with passion, joy, encouragement, and the power of choice coupled with health acceptance of what is.

Have you ever found that the more accepting you become and the less you resist and fight things, the less "bad" things keep happening to you? I have a teacher who says, "What you resist, persists." Therefore, this is an invitation to *force less; flow more.*

Start small here—you can only eat an elephant one bite at a time. Small, sustainable changes are the ones that actually last. If someone cuts you off in traffic, catch yourself before mindlessly responding with an expletive, and instead try laughing at the situation. Seriously! Maybe even provide an alternative explanation like, "Wow, they are so hyped up and stressed that they have to dart in front of me like that. No worries. I'm still here and doing fine," or "Maybe they're rushing to the hospital to see a loved one." You can scoff at this cliché example, but how many times have you become enraged when someone "wronged" you in traffic, allowing it to spin you out of control about things totally unrelated to the car in front of you? The thing is, it's not about you, and as soon as we realize that it's not always about us, acceptance starts coming much easier. It's a weight off. Really! Because being angry at the other person—or a situation you can't control, like a red light—doesn't change anything other than to put negative, unhealthy, unhappy energy inside you. Unfortunately, you end up hurting yourself and doing nothing to contribute to a positive outcome.

Can you transfer this lesson to something bigger? This is where the practice comes in. Maybe it's a bridge too far to let go of an abuse you suffered in a relationship. Okay. Start where you can. *Practice* letting go with the little things that you're not as attached to. It really will begin to build your "just roll with it" muscle.

In 2009, doctors discovered a tumor in my breast. They removed the tumor and had it biopsied. While I waited for the biopsy results, I admit I freaked out a little. I told myself it wasn't cancer, but deep down I was fearful it was. No matter the outcome, I decided to live my life and enjoy it, so I globetrotted through Europe for two months while I awaited the biopsy results. Through voracious reading, studying, and researching, in reflecting back on it, I believe that my stress and heartbreak were huge components of what caused that foreign growth in the first place. The test results finally came in and showed that the tumor was benign. I stayed in Europe for nearly a year, and I learned a valuable lesson about the importance of "letting go" and living a stress-free, joy-filled life.

In *Anatomy of the Spirit*, Dr. Carolyn Myss says, "Remaining attached to negative events and beliefs is toxic to our minds, spirits, cell tissue, and lives. Negative choices generate situations that recur in order to teach us how to make positive choices. Once we learn the lesson and make a positive choice, the situation does not recur because our spirit is no longer attached to the negative choice that gave rise to the lesson." What better reason do you need to let go of the past and just roll with it? Your life is literally on the line here. Can you trust yourself enough to heal yourself, or trust that something larger than you can heal you emotionally, physically, or spiritually? We must be healthy in order to heal, and being healthy will generate true happiness and success. But we have to start with a little drop of faith . . .

45

Having faith does not mean that everything coasts along in sunshine and butterfly land. Faith and healing are close sisters. And like sisters, sometimes they compete when it would be more helpful to recognize their differences and embrace those differences as supplemental and supportive, versus divisive. All that is to say that faith and healing allow space for mystery and curiosity too. Healing doesn't mean every ailment goes away and never comes back; healing may mean acceptance of where you are. Faith doesn't mean tough stuff stops happening; it means being present and purposeful day to day.

Difficult events won't ever stop happening because we are always growing, and like muscle tissue that tears when you lift weights then repairs and becomes stronger, we have to be torn apart in order to put ourselves back together to get our life education. What *can* change, though, is your attitude about those events. The space between stimulus and reaction (or response) contains choice. We have a choice about our relationship with unexpected bumps in the road. The very mind-set of acceptance, rooted in faith, will build a balanced and lasting character within the deepest layers of your soul.

Inevitably, we still find our lives out of balance, though, don't we? That is why it is imperative to embody the seven core character traits described throughout this book. Then, even if one part is missing from time to time, you can still roll with it. Ultimately, we aspire to find a lasting balance among all the character traits, but life will be life, and things will be bumpy, but you can keep rollin' if you've got a smooth, balanced wheel. This "wheel" is the SEMPER Philosophy and "Just Roll With It" Method of living a happy, healthy, and successful life of purpose.

Here's the wheel. Check it out.

## Why SEMPER and What Does it Mean?

"SEMPER" comes from *Semper Fidelis*, the motto of the United States Marine Corps, meaning "always faithful." In a narrow sense, *semper* simply means "always," but beyond that, in the SEMPER Philosophy, it means sustainable significance and purpose. SEMPER stands for always having faith, and always being Sincere, Empathetic, Motivated, Perseverant, Engaged and Excited, and Resilient.

After spending more than eight years dedicated to the United States Marine Corps, modifying the USMC motto of "Semper Fidelis" is incredibly apropos. I have joined my Just Roll With It Method and SEMPER attitude because I strive to *always* be myself. I strive for significance through authenticity while having faith that just rolling with it will best serve me and those with whom I interact. I have seen time and time again that I am happier and healthier living my life this way now. However, back in my military days, especially within an organization like the Marines, being an authentic version of myself was a more daunting task for a goofball girl like me than you might think. I struggled with *semper* being Sarah for a long time, which is why being genuine is a cornerstone of the life philosophy I apply to my leadership style, teamwork ethic, professional endeavors, spiritual life, and relationships today.

SEMPER represents sustainable significance because success is fleeting, yet *significance* is lasting. We want to cultivate something of significance within ourselves, for our lives, and as a legacy for our loved ones, right? Success should not just be a temporary condition. Knowing what real success means to you is imperative to actually finding that success. SEMPER success represents a deeper, healthier, happier, and more authentically abundant form of successful person who wants to contribute something positive to the world.

> *"The planet does not need more 'successful' people. But it does desperately need more peacemakers, healers, restorers, storytellers, and lovers of every shape and form. It needs people who live well in their places. It needs people of moral courage willing to join the fight to make the world habitable and humane. And these needs have little to do with success as our culture has defined it."*

—David Orr

During my time in the Marines, I witnessed both positive and negative examples of leadership and success principles, which I have embedded into (or left out of) what I now call the SEMPER Philosophy. Sometimes what the institution taught me was in line with my intuition; other times, the lessons I learned were how *not* to act. Thankfully, over time, I was able to create my *own* principles that carried me through the military, sports, education, and my relationships with integrity.

Also, I noticed something among most of my peers in all these endeavors; they pursued success, but not what I thought of as SEMPER success. They weren't seeking a lasting, significant, meaningful success that would not change as their rank, company, job title, or team status did. I am a social worker by trade and love to analyze human behavior.

What pressed on my heart, though, was that I wanted to teach this lifestyle to others. "Neither do people light a lamp and put it under a bowl. Instead they put it on its stand, and it gives light to everyone in the house" (Matthew 5:15). Also see Luke 11:33.

Are you aware and learning during your trials, or just a passive participant? You must be active! You must aspire to be a life-long student in all areas of your life. You must observe and learn and *own* your choices. Additionally, the story we craft for ourselves is our Divine footprint on this world. The soul within us all yearns to relate to others, to connect, to form relationships, and we do that through story. That is one huge element of our shared humanness. Stories can teach us lessons. Stories are powerful. Your story is powerful.

Okay, you get it. Maybe you're silently screaming, "Sarah, tell us already! How do we achieve this SEMPER success, this significance, this purpose?"

Let's take a look at the SEMPER Wheel again.

You may notice a piece in there that stands out from the others: Faith. Beyond the direct tie to the Marine Corps motto, *Semper Fidelis* (always faithful), being faithful is of paramount importance because of my personal, spiritual faith. This faith has been the central key to my growth, survival, health, happiness, and success. There is no way I would be alive today, experiencing the blessings I have, if it were not for my faith and trust in who Christ is, a God who loves me, the universe that conspires to give me the best life, and the love, support, and encouragement of others.

Time and time again, in war zones, back home, and on the athletic field, I was saved in ways that I attribute to the power of faith and an insurmountable spirit. The point is that I am not so happy because life has been easy for me; I am happy, deeply grateful for life, bursting with light and love for God and my friends and family *because of* the crap I have been through. I have an appreciation for life because I know how precious it is. I'll share more detail of some of these stories with you as a way to connect and to offer examples that are both similar to and different from yours.

Own your stories, too, and take heart in knowing future rewrites are possible.

My faith provided an avenue for me to choose that grateful mind-set. Gratitude gets my mind off my ego. I decided to see things as more than the immediate pain or pleasure and realize there was, and is, a bigger force at work in our lives. As I learned from one life lesson after another—the less I resisted, the less the bad things persisted. When I "let go and let God," my life became smoother.

> *"Peace. It doesn't mean to be in a place where there is no noise, trouble, or hard work. It means to be in the midst of those things and still be calm in your heart."*
>
> —Unknown

The smoothing out did not occur overnight. Eventually my life had more balance because I *chose* peace during times of chaos, *chose* acceptance over grief, and *chose* gratitude over grudge. I found that opening myself up to a higher power changed my relationship with stress; it did not prevent bad things from happening but helped me navigate the rough waters and finally find the shore. Will rough seas swell again? Of course, but faith is the foundation on which I rely. It is the central point to which I can return when I lose my way. It is my compass. It is my guiding light. It is my positive energy.

I believe in SEMPER success because it creates a *legacy*. To me, true success is based in faith and rooted in love, truth, and compassion toward ourselves and others. Typical, modern success is shallow and external when it emphasizes status over relationship, get-rich-quick instead of foundation and principle, and multitasking to try to one-up

51

your peers versus being fully present when you interact or work with someone. SEMPER success is significant and internal, targets your core, and gets people to believe in their purpose at a deeper level. I encourage you not to learn to be successful, but to be *significant* through SEMPER success no matter what tragedies you have experienced.

> *"Life is not about waiting for the storm to pass...it's about learning to dance in the rain."*
>
> —Vivian Greene

According to Dr. James Pawelski, there are six virtues and twenty-four signature strengths that are universally accepted as such no matter the historical point in time, culture, language, sex, or age. The six virtues (and twenty-four strengths) fit within the SEMPER framework in the following way:

» Faith—spirituality and open mindedness
» Sincere—integrity, humility/modesty, and self-regulation
» Empathetic—social intelligence, fairness, love, and kindness
» Motivated—leadership, appreciation of beauty and excellence, citizenship, and curiosity
» Perseverant—persistence, prudence, and creativity
» Engaged/Excited—vitality, humor, love of learning, and gratitude
» Resilient—hope, bravery, forgiveness and mercy, and perspective

Keep the traits, virtues, and signature strengths in mind while you evaluate the SEMPER Wheel framework. We are all naturally "SEMPER" at our core. We simply need to uncover it, accept it, and allow it to flow forth.

That said, take a moment to recognize that these traits, mind-sets, and behaviors exist along a spectrum, and none of these traits are inherently, or only and always, "good." SEMPER has a dark side too. Faith can be used to inspire, *or* it can be used to manipulate; sincerity can serve to connect, *or* it can exploit; empathy can restore hope, *or* it can deplete a spirit; motivation can guide, *or* it can blindly force; perseverance can focus our efforts, *or* end up blinding us to other options; engagement can build presence and mindfulness, *or* have us ignoring the consideration of others if we become self-absorbed; and resilience can provide a resurgence of strength, *or* cause us to never stop long enough to actually feel what we are going through.

Embracing both ends of the spectrum and everything in between, all elements of the SEMPER traits put "feel it, name it, own it, release it" into practice because we don't get to just play dumb or tune out the uncomfortable stuff. Here's what else (F)SEMPER can be:

» Faith—fear
» Sincerity—shame and needing to fit in
» Empathy—judgment
» Motivation—confusion
» Perseverance—complacency
» Engagement and excitement—disconnect and boredom/depression
» Resilience—defeat and hopelessness

They exist on a spectrum. Prepare to see, feel, taste, and become friends with all of this on the journey.

> *"If you wish to be a warrior prepare to get broken, if you wish to be an explorer prepare to get lost, and if you wish to be a lover prepare to be both."*
> —Daniel Saint

The SEMPER Wheel will be your visual "check-in" list moving forward. Before you read any further, I want you to take a few minutes to complete an exercise that will help you determine which traits are strengths and which are more challenging.

Start by taking a few slow breaths with your eyes closed, inhaling and exhaling through your nose. Settle in. Get comfortable. As your breath slows down, so will your thoughts. The body and mind are intimately connected. This simple breathing exercise will help you get what is often referred to as "centered." The basic act of deepening the breath and bringing more oxygen into your brain and body begins to heal you right away, just a little bit at a time, one . . . little . . . breath . . . at a time. You can do it.

The SEMPER Wheel has seven sections: six traits around the wheel and one circle in the middle. Look at each wedge-shaped section representing the traits and place a dot within each section marking how satisfied you are with each one in your life. A dot placed close to the middle of the circle indicates dissatisfaction or feeling that it is a weak area in your life, while a dot placed on the periphery indicates ultimate satisfaction. When you have a placed a dot in each wedge, connect the dots to see your circle of SEMPER. With the faith circle in the middle, shade the circle in completely if you feel full of faith and strong in your spiritual life; fill it in less if faith has less of an influence in your life or you feel it is an area in which you struggle. This is a simple activity, but can lead to profound growth if you take it seriously.

You now have a clear visual representation of any imbalances in your core traits, providing a starting point for determining where you may wish to spend more time and energy to create balance and strength in your life. This wheel can be used to make an overall assessment of your current state of being, and it can also be used to aid in decision making in specific circumstances.

Happiness, health, and success take time. Don't worry about perfecting everything today, this week, this month, or this year. You *can* do it all, but you don't have to do it all *now*. This is a *practice*!

Likewise, we need a challenge to keep us engaged. You need to challenge yourself to make the *big* changes, for those are the ones that ignite a spark within your spirit to live life to your fullest capacity and purpose. Start with the smallest movement forward that gets the ball rolling. Generate some momentum.

Sure, you will make mistakes along the way, and that's fine. Just keep moving forward. Stumbling is part of the process of growth. As the infamous General George S. Patton said, "If a man does his best, what else is there?" Strive for excellence, not perfection.

Can we begin to have a gentler and more accepting attitude even in tumultuous situations? Can we see if our pain, frustration, or stress starts to decrease even a little bit if we shift our mind-sets in healthy ways? I'm willing to bet that we can, because as we begin a letting go, as we *surrender*, we allow a filling up, and life becomes a whole new journey on which to embark.

*"You can clutch your past so tightly to your chest that it leaves your arms too full to embrace the present."*

—Jan Glidewell

## OFFERING: Prayer or Meditation

(Remember, this is all a practice!)
- » "Dear God, empower me to force less and flow more."
- » Or, in mantra (repetition) form: "Force less. Flow more."
- » "Feel it. Name it. Own it. Release it."
- » "Let go. Let God."

# Chapter 3

# FAITH

F" is for faith—the cog in the SEMPER Wheel, because our faith is our foundation from which all else grows. As humans, we are hard wired for connection to something bigger than ourselves and to a carving out of and living up to our deep purpose.

Faith is about relationship, and faith is a practice—something to be experienced and lived out. We don't just *feel* faith; we can *live* it!

Research on religion and health, and the personal stories of many of us, points toward the truism that God matters to us. Whether it's Brené Brown asserting that spirituality kept coming up in her research as a requirement for "Whole-Hearted Living," Duke University's combination of religion and health sciences research indicating the way faith-affiliation and practice impact health, or resilience studies continuing to show the power of connectedness, we cannot ignore the fact that connection with God is what we're wired for.

*Be on your guard; stand firm in the faith; be courageous; be strong. Do everything in love.*

—1 Corinthians 16:13–14

## What Is the Essence of Faith?

» love
» trust
» hope

» grace and gratitude
» devotion to that with which you are aligned
» spirituality
» connection
» loyalty and honor

*"It seems that gratitude without practice may be a little like faith without works – it's not alive."*

—Brené Brown, *The Gifts of Imperfection*

## What Does Faith in Action Look Like?

» service
» generosity
» gratitude
» surrender
» acceptance
» reaching out to others as well as receiving help from others
» letting go of certainty
» embracing mystery

"Without exception, spirituality—the belief in connection, a power greater than self, and the interconnections grounded in love and compassion—emerged as a component of resilience," says Brené Brown in regards to her decade plus of research about shame, vulnerability, joy, and the living of a "wholehearted life." Admittedly, allowing a letting go of control or the things we're habitually used to clinging to is difficult because we're creatures who seek comfort in the tried and true. Yet, there's a sense of freedom that arises when we accept the mystery within faith and accept each moment as being exactly what we need at that point in our walk of life. It allows for a release of the weight of having to figure it all out ourselves and welcomes in surprises. It allows life to be a teacher, not just something happening to us.

Ultimately, faith empowers us to cultivate a life of purpose, which is what we all want. The letting go, surrender, and acceptance makes space for things much bigger and brighter than we could ever imagine on our own.

Faith is dynamic and diverse, though, too. Within faith, we wrestle with doubt. We wrestle with fear. It requires courage to admit that we don't know what we don't know all the time. This is a place where we can very practically apply acceptance if we are able to acknowledge, name, and be present with the fact that just because we doubt and worry and become scared at times does not mean we are not faithful. All that dark stuff is wrapped up in the light stuff too.

Faith, as ethereal as it often seems, is also very much about the power of our own thoughts. Believe that there's enough faith, love, patience, grace, (or whatever!) to go around. There isn't a finite amount of it, and we all have the birthright to live and breathe our own faith every day. When we offer up gratitude, we are practicing faith, and we are sending out the signal, "Yes please, God, I want more of this."

Whether through prayer, meditation, other mindfulness practices, or some combo of all of those, the energy of faith we generate in those moments is for real! So send up those prayers, allow for the details to unfold in a way you may not have designed yourself, and choose to be patient and joyful in the process. Wait for the gift to unfold before your eyes (even if it's not packaged the way you wanted it to be!). Choosing to love and trust is the first step we take toward being free enough to fly again.

> *"She went out on a limb, had it break off behind her, and discovered she could fly."*
>
> —Kobi Yamada, "She"

Faith first became a critical element of my worldview the summer between my sophomore and junior years of college, and it came through connection with others. It started rather painfully, though, when I tore my left hamstring on the first day of Air Force Reserve Officer Training Corps (ROTC) Field Training at Lackland Air Force Base in San Antonio, Texas. I limped through training for a week before I finally accepted that I would rather go home and come back the next summer healthy than perform at a mediocre level during the four weeks of training I'd been looking forward to for so long. (Yup, I was twisted in college and liked to get yelled at and throw my body around on obstacle courses.)

Because I left training early, the remainder of my summer suddenly opened up, and I had the opportunity to meet up with one of my best childhood friends, Tori. She was notoriously Christian and I was a full-fledged skeptic/borderline-atheist/raised-Catholic/I'm-too-full-of-guilt-to-believe-much-of-anything type of kid at the time. So when I called Tori and told her I was unexpectedly in Georgia at home with my parents (instead of in Texas at Air Force training), and found out she was home with her parents in South Carolina, she invited me to drive north and visit her.

The day I'd arrive was a Friday. She regularly attended a Friday night Bible study. She invited me to join her, and I was as shocked as she was when I said yes.

I knew Tori had strong Christian beliefs. Often, after talking on the phone for an hour, during which I would usually describe some life dilemma with drama and (what I thought was) flair, she would end the conversation with, "All right, I'm praying for you. Love you!" I'd always laugh and think, "Ya, okay, whatever. I don't even know what that means, but thanks. And what does praying for me have to do with what I was just talking about?" So, I wasn't surprised that hitting up a Bible study was what she'd be up to on a Friday night. My typical auto-response would have been "Thanks, but no thanks," but that day I threw my eyebrows up, shrugged my shoulders, and said "Sure, I'll go."

I arrived at Tori's home in Sumter, South Carolina, just in time to drop my bags then jump in her silver Civic and head to aforementioned Bible study.

I expected a formal church atmosphere because my only exposure to religion was that of Catholic Mass, so when the door to the hosts' home swung open and hugs were exchanged with perfect strangers, I was suspicious. The host couple guided us through the hallway where the back part of the house opened into adjoining family room, kitchen, and living room filled with young adults. People were on the floor, the couches, loitering and talking, and there was some hugging and crying happening too. It looked like a commune to me.

Soon after we arrived, dinner was served. A long, informal prayer preceded the feast. We held hands. There were lots of "my Lords" and "God, please, just this" or "please, just that" and "Jesus, I love you." What kind of prayer was this? I cheated and peeked through my loosely closed lids. Apparently, I was the only one scrunching my brow over this entreaty.

The sermon ended, eyes flew open, and food was passed from right to left. The dinner table hummed with conversation throughout the meal. In true commune fashion, everyone lent a hand in the cleaning-up process, and soon we were all seated in a circle on the floor. Most people had Bibles in their laps, notebooks, pens, and looked like they were at a collegiate lecture. I likely made the same face I made at the dinner table as I re-observed my peers.

Again, we bowed our heads and held hands. Formality never appeared. The adults read from the Bible, explaining each line of the chosen passage. People asked questions. We discussed. More questions were posed, prayers were beseeched, and everyone got to say something on the topic at hand. People my age, not quite kids but not "real" adults yet either, stuttered through tears as they gave mini-confessions or implored with their words sincerity I'd never seen before. My disdain faded over the course of the hours we spent in that home. Although many members present were moved to tears before the night was over, everyone seemed . . . well, *happy.*

We got back in that silver Civic, and as the car door shut another one opened. A floodgate of comments and questions burst forth from me the entire drive home. When we got to Tori's house, we sat on the couch and the conversation continued for hours. I was amazed by the way everyone had prayed that night. What *was* it? It didn't sound like *anything* I'd ever heard before. And people didn't seem like they'd been dragged there against their will. People loitered and talked afterward, asking about each other's lives in, what appeared to me, a very genuine manner. I wanted to know the cause of all that warmth. I wanted an explanation for the connection amongst everyone there.

Tori answered every question I had, never seeming tired even though it was past midnight. When I ran out of technical questions, I had a request.

What happened next surprised me even more than my original "yes" to attend the Friday night Bible study. I scooted forward on the couch, fell to my knees, and felt as though God was there beside me in that room, with His hand on my shoulder, pushing me toward the floor, gently. From my knees, I leaned forward, my hands bracing myself as I lay prostrate, pouring out tears I didn't know were at the ready.

"I want to *believe*."

There are few people in this world I know now who could've handled that situation as beautifully as Tori did. "Sarah?"

"I want to know what it means to believe," I managed to whisper again between the tears.

"Oh, Sarah! I'm so happy!" Tori's huge smile hugged me, and in an instant those tears of aching turned to ones of joy. "Sarah, Jesus is so cool. You're going to love Him so much!"

I told her I didn't know how to pray. That felt like a starting point— talking to God—and I didn't know how.

"Just talk to Him like a person, Sarah. You don't need to be formal. He just wants to hear from you in whatever way you can manage to speak to Him."

"Really?!"

"Yup."

"Well, Tori, there's something else." How would I say this? I had joked about the idea so much over the past year and half that it didn't feel real to me. "I'm not supposed to be in the Air Force, Tori. I'm supposed to be in the Marine Corps. I feel like God is telling me *right now* that *that* is where I'm supposed to be. It's like He literally snapped my hamstring in half in order to get my attention, to tell me '*You are not supposed to be here.*' But I can't. With a retired Air Force Colonel as a father and a mother who doesn't really think women should be in the military, my family will be pissed, and the Air Force will say no because I'm on scholarship and have already committed my time in serve to them. But I know, I just *know*, I have to be in the Marines."

"Wow, Sarah! That is incredible! God is speaking to you through your heart. That is what it means to have a relationship with God."

Something inexplicable changed in me that evening. The other students at the Bible study, the mentors, the teachers, and the fellowship all tore down an internal wall I did not even know I had up. While Tori and I sat on the couch in her parents' living room, I felt an internal flood rising up within me and something or someone brought me to my hands and knees, and words I never thought I would utter came pouring out of my mouth. "I want to know what it means to believe." I had studied religion academically in college and had convinced myself I did so for the historical and sociological perspective. There, that summer night, though, the invitation came from my *heart*. I wanted to *know* and *live* faith.

That was the beginning of my ever-changing rising and falling walk with God. That summer was a major turning point in my life. When I returned to the University of Virginia, I told my Air Force ROTC commander, a full-bird colonel (which means he's kind of a big deal), that I had to be a Marine. He said no. I spent a year in heated negotiations with the Air Force, Marines, and Navy to make the switch a reality. The Air Force thought they were calling my bluff, claiming I only wanted to be a Marine because of my jarhead buddies. The Marines extended their hand and began to train me before knowing how things would pan out.

Although I put everything in my twenty-year-old life on the line—losing my full scholarship through AFRTOC, being threatened with getting kicked out of college and enlistment in the Air Force (and having to pay back everything the Air Force had already invested in my education), disappointing my parents, suffering more physical injuries—I had never been more certain of a decision in my life because of the steadfastness of my belief in a calling.

Belief is only part of my story. I now see that decision I made in 2001, and faith in general, less as belief and more as surrendering and trusting in a higher power. Can you actively "let go and let God" do the work in your life? Faith means relinquishing that delusionary feeling of control. When we attempt to control everything around us, we are acting out of fear of the unknown, right? When we make choices based on fear, we basically slap Divine guidance in the face and say, "No thanks, God, that's not for me." But things keep happening—coincidences, mysteries, surprises—because we are meant to realize the limitation of our own power and rely on a Source greater than ourselves.

As Dr. Carolyn Myss says in *Anatomy of the Spirit*, "Surrender to Divine authority means liberation from physical illusions, not from the delights and comfort of physical life . . . [There is a] difference between surrender and resignation . . . Saying yes to our condition is the first part—an act that may or may not change our condition—and saying yes to God's timing is the second." Recognizing our own limitations and trusting God out of a sense of faith, not obligation or resignation, is crucial to being in tune with His gifts and operating your life from a place of heart and soul, which has the capacity to impact the rest of the world. Faith isn't even just about you because living in a faith-filled, passionate way enables you to be a light to others in this world too, and God knows the world needs your light.

> *"Dare to reach out your hand into the darkness, to pull another hand into the light."*
>
> —Norman B. Rice

Faith is more than a feeling and a belief; it's an action. Faith is a practice. Faith is something to return to, to doubt, and to return again.

In 2013, I was asked to speak at Hanuman Festival in Boulder, Colorado, about "What Are You Devoted To?" And the question I asked myself in answer to their question was, "If I'm devoted to something, it means I'm living it faithfully, imperfectly practicing it as best as I can as often as I can. So, how do I *practice* my faith?" One word kept coming back to me: service.

This is an excerpt from my speech notes for that presentation:

I am devoted to service because it is love and faith in action, service reminds me that self-care is not selfish, and service empowers me to force less, flow more, and ultimately just roll with it!

First, my definition of service existed mainly in a military context for me because I grew up in a military family, then I served in the military myself.

Then, service as love and faith existed within Christian definitions as I transitioned from being nearly atheist to a "believer" about ten years ago and thinking of serving Christ as my main purpose.

I found that service in the military sense, then faith-based sense, then personal and professional sense, and now more than ever truly spiritual sense, is my absolute driving purpose in life. No matter how it's defined, it's still about service for me.

Because service ultimately means love in action, and love is truly the root of it all.

Every major world philosophy or religion says something to the effect of "To love is Divine" or "God is love." I believe that love is our essence, our oneness, and a pathway to express that love is through service.

*"Each of you should use whatever gift you have received to serve others, as faithful stewards of God's grace in its various forms."*
—1 Peter 4:10

Trust, patience, and acceptance are siblings of faith because patience requires trust and trust is built on faith. Behaving in an impatient way indicates a mistrust that things will not happen as they should and you feel compelled to (try to) control them according to your plan even when everything else around you is telling you to slow down, wait, be patient.

Moreover, in no way am I implying that faith *prevents* challenging things from happening; being faith-filled just means you will have a different, more centered, more accepting perspective on things when you do hit a bump in the road. Challenges serve to wake us up! Can we accept the challenge?

As we surrender, we open up a space for God to fill us up in ways we could have never imagined on our own. When our faith deepens in this way, we find that we no longer feel the need to control everything, because we see things evolving as they should. As you embrace what—slowly but surely—becomes a natural unfolding of blessings, you are bound to find the happiest, most fulfilling, and most rewarding moments of your life. Have faith and the rest will flow.

Faith is not an insurance policy. We don't get more God, more faith, and more spirit by trying harder; we get it through surrender. Faith doesn't happen through our greatest effort and our biggest successes. Heaven happening now is the Divine living within us, through us, and as I heard a minister once say, "The less of you, the more room for God."

Faith is coming to the edge of light and waiting expectantly for more light.

The key is *PRACTICE*. We must practice exercising our "spiritual muscle."

Faith—like love—is great to feel, but it becomes transformative and powerful when it is *done*, when it is put into ACTION.

Faith—like love—is a verb.

Faith—like love—is enhanced with gratitude.

Faith—like love—is meant to be experienced.

Faith—like love—is limitless.

Faith—like love—exists along a spectrum. Faith includes doubt, fear, and insecurity. Faith becomes richer, I think, when we embrace all elements of it.

Faith—like love—can sometimes be the belief in things unseen, intangible, and indefinable, from God to your belief in your ability to do a handstand, when you've never done one before in your life, and everything in between.

Faith—like love—involves trust and unknowing and surrender. It is choosing to see the beauty within the mystery.

Faith . . . *is* love?

What do you think?

What is *faith*? And how do you *practice* it?

# Roll Call: Faith

*You, my brothers and sisters, were called to be free. But do not use your freedom to indulge the flesh; rather, serve one another humbly in love.*

—Galatians 5:13

1. Who are your faith "roll" models? What about them do you admire?
2. What defines a happy, healthy, and connected sense of faith to you?
3. What does it mean to *live* faithfully? Has there been a time in your life when you have lived in faith, or a time when you lived from a place of doubt? How were those times different? How did you feel? Describe it here.

4. What would you need to do to improve and deepen the faith of your relationship with yourself, with others, and with something larger than yourself?

5. How do you feed your soul? Be honest about what's distracting you from or separating you from God. Have you made space for spirit in your life? If not, what are you filling that space with instead?

6. Rolling with faith: Faith is not necessarily the absence of fear, but the courage to think, believe, and act in a spirit of trust despite that fear. Eventually, deep faith releases fear and puts it all in the hands of the Divine. Let go, and let God.

# OFFERING: Prayer or Meditation

» The Serenity Prayer

God, give me grace to accept with serenity
the things that cannot be changed,
Courage to change the things
which should be changed,
and the Wisdom to distinguish
the one from the other.

Living one day at a time,
Enjoying one moment at a time,
Accepting hardship as a pathway to peace,
Taking, as Jesus did,
This sinful world as it is,
Not as I would have it,
Trusting that You will make all things right,
If I surrender to Your will,
So that I may be reasonably happy in this life,
And supremely happy with You forever in the next.
Amen.

» Inhale "let," exhale "go." Repeat.

# Chapter 4

# SINCERE

*"When you are content simply to be yourself and don't compare or compete, everyone will respect you."*

—Lao-tzu

## What Is the Essence of Sincerity?

- » Free of deceit or hypocrisy
- » Genuine
- » Real
- » Pure
- » Authentic
- » Honest
- » Worthy of trust
- » Unpretentious
- » Heartfelt
- » Humble
- » Accepting of your unique qualities, as well as your imperfections

*"This side of Paradise, it is our business (not, like so many, peddlers of God's word but as men and women of sincerity) to speak with our hearts (which is what sincerity means) and to bear witness to, and live out of, and live toward, and live by, the true word of His holy story as it seeks to stammer itself forth through the holy stories of us all."*

—Frederick Buechner

# What Does Sincerity in Action Look Like?

» Courageously living from a place of love, honesty, and vulnerability
» Making choices based on intuition
» Engaging your beliefs and actions in congruence
» Living with integrity
» Communicating with forthrightness with yourself and others about your truth, your strengths, and your weaknesses
» Owning your own story
» Delivering on promises to yourself and others
» Dropping the perfectionism act
» Trusting yourself and feeling safe within yourself
» Accepting yourself as the unique person that you are

*"What a man thinks of himself, that is which determines, or rather indicates, his fate."*

—Henry David Thoreau

During my first deployment to Iraq, although I was already well equipped with a couple dozen nicknames, I acquired a slew of new ones while living in the desert: Susie Q, Pep Rally, Dusty, and Wonder Kid. Pep Rally (or "PR" for short) was the one that stuck because, as some said, I seemed to be the happiest Marine in Iraq. *Happy* is a relative term. I wouldn't self-ascribe my emotional state that way at all times during those seven months. Yet I *was* very peppy during most of that deployment.

I am naturally sarcastic and sophomoric, so in that regard, the Marines was a good fit. The cheeriness that often accompanied my jokes, the smiles I displayed on a daily basis, and the egalitarian way in which I led my Marines didn't quite fit the Marine mold. As early into my Marine Corps career as Officer Candidates School (OCS) training, my sergeant instructors implored, "Plummer, why you always laughin'?!" And three years after OCS, during my time in Iraq, my Commanding Officer (CO) told me I smiled too much.

Every day on my first deployment, that one CO would walk past my desk and either tell me to shut up (before I even said anything), knock something off my desk (plastic reindeer that pooped jelly beans, ridiculous beanie babies, dinosaur-shaped sponges), or just glare at me. I swore he was on a mission to tear me down and I didn't know why.

Some days it got to me, and I'd vow to remain dejected all day long, believing that my surly countenance would somehow hurt *his* feelings. I would tell myself, "Don't smile at anyone today. Don't crack one single joke so that jerk won't have any reason to cut me down." It almost never lasted though. Someone would toss out a "soft-ball" comment, prompting me to throw in a "that's what she said," and the whole command center would ripple with laughter.

On the good days, the days when I was rooted in a sincere sense of self, I would embark on a personal mission to show him he couldn't break me and I'd be damn happy whether he wanted me to be or not. I armed myself for battle against "the man" by telling jokes, making gift baskets for the Marines who weren't getting care packages from home, spending one-on-one time advising my Marines, and mentoring the handful of young enlisted Marines from other sections of the unit who were "out" Christians in the squadron (and were berated by the others because of it). I was going to be Pep Rally whether he liked it or not, dammit. And seemingly, clearly he did *not* like it, not one bit.

Seven months later, just as we were getting ready to head back home to the US, the CO pulled me into his office one afternoon and said, "Plummer, we need to talk." I thought for sure I was about to get another lecture about needing to be more "professional"—otherwise known as needing to become a "robot" in my opinion. So, I settled into the office chair on the other side of his desk and braced for impact. I wasn't prepared, however, for what he said next. "You single-handedly raised the morale of this entire unit during the deployment." He paused. "Thank you." I remained glued to my seat.

"Thank you, sir." It probably sounded more like a question than a statement.

Then he said, "Get out."

I didn't dare smile in front of him then, but as soon as I was out of eyesight, a grin painted my face and my thoughts began spinning. It had come full circle: I had (for the most part) remained true to myself, and it had paid off in the end. As much as I hated the treatment I received most days there, those few, positive words that the CO had uttered to me remained with me more than any of his negative ones. Furthermore, the feedback I received from the Marines in my section, as well as from those in other sections, made being myself—and subsequently, often being ridiculed for doing so—all worth it in the end.

Isn't it exhausting when you spend time trying to be someone else? So, let's stop faking it and just be ourselves already, people! As Eleanor Roosevelt famously said, "Do what you feel in your heart to be right, for you'll be criticized anyway."

I encourage you to consider this: set your goal, your aim, or your concern in any given situation toward that of being authentic versus being liked, or worrying about what people think. Being authentic is a goal you can *actually* attain; being liked by everyone probably is not. Man, that takes a weight off, don't you think? That means now I can walk into a studio to teach an all-levels yoga class and strive to do my best (not be "perfect"), and to be genuine (not hope everyone loves my class and if everyone doesn't then clearly it means I am a bad person and a terrible teacher), and I can live with the outcome. Moreover, I can feel "accomplished" because I was authentic and any compliments that follow are a bonus! And, yes, of course, those bonuses *do* feel good and can be affirming to my work, yet I'm likely to be less and less in a state of *requiring* them for validation.

Closely related to sincerity and authenticity are integrity and intuition. *Integrity* is a word that gets thrown around a lot in schools, training environments, and in the workplace. At the University of Virginia, there was a strict honor code that dictated the expulsion of students if they were in violation of any of the rules mandating integrity. Likewise, in the Marines, the slogan "honor, courage, commitment" is etched on walls and is a mantra in most professional settings. Yet, the deeper sense of the word is often missed. Significant integrity is a matter of being *whole*, and wholeness includes the duality within us all: the good and the bad, the joy and fear. Integrity is so much more than not cheating or not stealing; it's about doing what you say you'll do and being candid about the times you haven't. Integrity is integrating your beliefs, words, actions, and habits. It's about the *congruence* of your convictions and your behavior, yet it allows for making mistakes and still maintaining integrity by being honest with yourself and others about your shortcomings.

Living honorably and being sincere does not mean being "perfect." In order to be sincere, we must be truthful with ourselves and with others. A mentor of mine and accomplished leadership consultant, M. J. Clark, says, "We must strongly believe in our abilities, but we must also appear real and human and fallible to those who follow. We will make mistakes. And that's okay; it's necessary for our ultimate success." I totally agree!

This is precisely what encourages me to remember—as I mentioned with faith, as well—that sincerity is a *practice*. Sincerity is not something we're born with or without; it's something we can choose, cultivate, and practice. We must nurture and grow our sincerity garden, not neglect is and starve it and expect to bear authentic fruit.

I have had people ask me why they should bother being genuine. They argue that they need to fit in professionally or they will be penalized, for instance. My answer is that because the benefits of being genuine, whether for self-serving *or* selfless reasons, are innumerable. It's kind of like when you're upset and someone tells you just to smile anyway because it tricks your brain into being happy. If you set out to be more authentic, thinking it will serve you better, make you more successful, or make more people like you, it turns out, you'll end up being a better version of yourself by default, and that more candid version of yourself is better for everyone else around you too. Plus, sincerity is contagious!

Sincerity's opposite is contagious also. If you perform as a half-hearted, half-truth version of yourself in any area of your life, it will begin to eat away at you eventually. The life you thought you had (professionally, personally, spiritually, and physically) will actually begin to falter, fade, and fall apart. Simply put, there is no other way to a significant, *real* life, than to live it authentically. We cannot live apart from our true selves.

And here's the great thing: most of the time you don't have to make any special effort to "do" anything, because simply living authentically is inspiring in and of itself. It gives permission to others to live authentically too.

*"The only relationship you can control is the one with yourself. What lies behind us, and what lies before us, are tiny matters when compared to what lies within us."*

—Ralph Waldo Emerson

So, I mentioned integrity and intuition a few paragraphs back. Now, here's the scoop on intuition, which I think of as a foundational component of sincerity: it is about knowing what you know. Intuition is about "gut feeling," right? Well, it's also about knowing what you *don't* know. As all these traits do, intuition, too, exists on a spectrum that includes positive and negative qualities, or even kind of an "abundant" and "lacking" quality. But instead of believing those ends of the spectrum to be oppositional to one another, the more we see them as complementary, the more they can work to our benefit. Here's what I mean: intuition is all the ways we know what we know *and* all the times we can admit we don't know and need more information (versus forcing our way through a situation).

One other story of sincerity is the one in which I'm currently engaged: "Yogini" vs. "Marine." Plus throw "Christian" into the mix. Oh boy. This feels a little messy to me at times. I came from a world of hierarchy, open displays of brute strength, and an environment of conformity. I left the Marines, and three years later obtained my Yoga Teacher certification. I often teach yoga to active duty service members, military veterans, and their families. When I engage with veterans in volunteer settings and professional realms now, I frequently meet raised eyebrows and sideways glances. There are a variety of reasons why those people end up taking a class with me, and it's not always voluntary.

Recently, I was consulting and teaching for a large military veteran nonprofit organization. Part of the mindfulness and resiliency training programming I was there to provide included yoga classes in the morning. The warriors had been told ahead of time that yoga was part of the programming. So, on the first day, in typical military fashion of "hurry up and wait," the group of participants and teacher loitered outside the office before loading into the vans to drive to the retreat site. Most of the men smoked and talked to one another in pairs, or stayed solo and spit their dip juice into the grass.

One gentleman in his late 30s approached me.

"So, I heard we're doing yoga on this trip," he said.

"Yup," I said.

I'd already been the butt of various yoga jokes as soon as the incoming warriors identified me as said yoga teacher.

"Well, I have religious objections to doing yoga," he continued.

"Okay." I waited. "And would you like to tell me what those are."

"I'm a Christian."

Another long pause. I had a cross necklace on. I pointed at it.

"So am I. Can you be more specific so I can better understand your perspective?"

The gentleman proceeded to list reasons I hadn't ever quite heard before and, frankly, that weren't congruent with how I have learned yoga, been taught by others, or currently teach to students. I explained some of those differences to him, as well as what my approach would be. He told me that if it was "just fancy stretching" then he would give it a try.

To his credit, the next morning, he was there on his yoga mat in the front row. He approached me after class. I asked him, "How'd it go?"

He said, "Well, I really liked it until at the end when you told us to empty our souls and replace it with something that's not God."

As far as I know, I kept a straight face.

"I believe what I said was to return to your safe space that I cued you toward at the beginning of class."

He didn't hear me.

I asked the other staff members if they'd heard me say anything even remotely close to what the gentleman claimed I'd said. They burst out laughing and assured me I hadn't.

But again, to his credit, he was on his mat again the next morning to try it out.

Look, I used to be a yoga skeptic too. I actually got kicked out of classes because I wouldn't shut up or stop laughing! I hated yoga. It hurt. I thought it was goofy. People seemed too "soft" to me. I was also skeptical because I thought it might degrade my faith.

That's cool. Faith is multifaceted and also involves being curious. Faith does not have to be blind. That gentleman actually did precisely what I encourage others to do when starting yoga. Take it if you like it and leave behind whatever doesn't make sense to you, for you right now.

Question everything. (Yes, even ME!).

Only do things that resonate with you. (Sometimes you have to try it first to know. Then, try it again another time.)

Don't do something that feels forced or fake.

Ask questions.

Try it at home.

Try different teachers.

Try different studios.

Be curious.

Just breathe.

Just roll with it.

Basically, whether it be trying yoga or trying a new food, be sincere about the endeavor.

I'm clearly not going to win every veteran over with yoga. I can live with that, though, when I remember my goal is to be authentic, honest, and congruent, and that I actually hope for and expect the same from others. So if someone is skeptical, good on 'em! Asking questions is good!

My friend, Kris Beal, wrote a blog called "The Messy Side of Being Brave." It eloquently encapsulates many principles of sincerity we've discussed already, because sincerity *is* so often a messy and courageous journey, and so I wanted to share part of it with you.

She says, "I had this unexpected thought process the other day. It started with dreams of more travel. One thing led to another, and my roller bag became a backpack. My spa accommodations turned into a hostel. My ticket suddenly become one way. I saw it all perfectly and my habitual thoughts of 'You can't do that!' were replaced immediately by 'But of course I can do that. I am brave!'"

Out of nowhere. I am brave. What a simple and powerful truth.

Upon further reflection, I remembered that I have a lifetime of courageous acts.

At seventeen, when I missed the scheduled rendezvous with my college buddies in Barcelona, I decided to punt and travel Europe alone. That was brave.

In 1988, I entered a room full of strangers and told them that I was an alcoholic and needed help. That was brave.

I told my scary ex-husband, "Enough." That was brave.

I've told these (and other) stories dozens of times using different descriptors—desperate, naïve, silly, young, dumb, broken. But I never used the word *brave* to describe myself. So when that deep truth washed over me, I took it all in and smiled.

What's interesting about these examples is that it was never pretty. In each instance, it was messy, vaguely incoherent, nauseating, teary, and always gut wrenching.

Today's small acts and words take on a subtler tone, but they are no less brave.

I tell the truth about myself.

I sit with my discomfort in stillness.

I try new things that I'm not good at.

I had forgotten that traveling solo to Costa Rica, New York City, Mont Tremblant, Big Sur, Joshua Tree, and Atlanta was brave, until a friend reminded me.

Ahhh . . . how easily I dismiss the stronger aspects of my being.

Contemplation: What does courage look like on you? What were the results? How did it make you feel? Is there something now that warrants a bit more bravery today? What are the thoughts or feelings blocking you?"

I really appreciate Kris's raw sincerity in this piece. It gives me permission to own some of my own braveness too, because you know what? I'm brave for teaching yoga to veterans. It doesn't matter that I am a veteran too. We can be a scary bunch sometimes! And to be honest, there are days that I question whether or not I should keep doing that, or if I should stick with just teaching yoga to the people who want more yoga. Then, I remember that it's not about me anyway. What is sincere for me is that I know yoga has the capacity to heal; so I'll live with the criticism and keep on going doing the work that needs to be done. It won't work well or jibe with everyone, and that's okay; for those for whom it can be a conduit to healing, then what a blessing that I might get to be a part of facilitating that in some way. Lastly, I remember what

Joseph Campbell is often quoted as saying, that "The privilege of a lifetime is being who you are." Heck yeah!

Sincerity and gratitude connect us to the Divine. Gratitude for our original experience, although it's always changing, it is ours from present moment to present moment and equips us to be the authentic authors of our very own stories. No one else can be who we are, so let's get busy living us!

If you're looking for some more reasons to justify a sincere lifestyle, here you go:

1. Living a fake version of ourselves is absolutely toxic to our system. Being a phony will negatively affect every aspect of our lives. Don't think so? "Fake the funk." When we pretend to be someone we are not, it's only a matter of time before we feel like we're rotting from the inside out. Frankly, life is easier living from our true spirit and personality. Let's not waste time and energy trying to be something we are not.

2. Living as the true version of you subsequently creates a cleaner, more confident you. Living from a place of authenticity boosts our self-reliance, automatically making us inspiring and attractive on a mental, physical, and spiritual level. No one wants to be in a relationship with a fake. Heck, even YOU don't want to be in a relationship with a fake you, why would someone else want to be? You naturally form better connections and grow healthier relationships by being your "true you."

3. Becoming more real means becoming more attune to our intuition and gut. Making smart decisions becomes a more easeful process because plugging into our intuition empowers us to make better choices about EVERYTHING. For instance, you may find that you make shifts in your career fields more toward something that feels like the one you feel *called to* be in, you find yourself dating a person with whom you feel more aligned, and you even do the workouts and eat the foods that are truly the best fit for you. The concept of "bioindividuality"— what works for one, may not work for another—applies to mental, physical, and spiritual nutrition; let's *feed* ourselves according to *our* needs.

4.  Being sure of who we are allows us to create healthier boundaries and tune out the haters, naysayers, and energy vampires way better than we could before. Life becomes less distracting as we become "centered" on who we really are. Life becomes calmer, smoother, and easier in many ways.

5.  We feel respect for ourselves and see it mirrored by others.

6.  It isn't just about you. St. Teresa of Avila said: Settle yourself in solitude, and you will come upon God in yourself. When we quiet the mind long enough, we find the Divine within our true self as well. Being sincere isn't just about our relationship with others, and ourselves, by the way; it's about our relationship with our God, Creator, and Source. As we tap into that relationship, we begin experiencing a whole new level of joy we may have never thought was possible before.

7.  Being sincere sometimes means that we'll be unpopular. Guess what? That's okay! Open up to the possibility that it might actually be the best gift of our lives to do something "unpopular" and not the dreadful thing we imagine it to be. We may, in fact, end up inspiring ourselves and our friends along the way simply by stepping forward and doing our own thing. We inadvertently give permission to others to live their lives more authentically too.

8.  We get to drop the "perfection" baggage. (Hooray!) While living authentically, we drop the illusion of being perfect, we begin to trust ourselves, accept ourselves as the unique people that we are, and have the courage to act according to what our intuition tells us. One of the main things we lose after trauma is our intuition, but we deserve to get it back and it is possible to do so. "The thing that is really hard, and really amazing, is giving up on being perfect and beginning the work of becoming yourself." Anna Quindlen

9.  Being sincere is more peaceful. When we are in-process, comparing our middle to someone else's end can be downright demoralizing. As we accept our own authentic present state of things, though, we invite a lot more ease into our lives.

10. We get to feel safe within ourselves. Sincerity is very closely tied to our sense of safety. We can't live sincerely if we feel unsafe, and we can't feel safe if we live insincerely.

*"The moment you accept yourself as you are, all burdens, mountainous burdens simply disappear. Then life is a sheer joy."*

—Bhagwan Shree Rajne

# Roll Call: Sincerity

*"If I really want to improve my situation, I can work on the one thing over which I have control—myself."*

—Stephen R. Covey

1. Who are your sincerity "roll" models? What about them do you admire?
2. Describe a time in your life in which you lived authentically. And how about a time when you didn't?
3. What defines a happy and connected sense of sincerity to you?
4. What would you have to do to improve and deepen the sincerity of your relationship with yourself? With others?
5. What is one specific situation in which you can set an authenticity goal?
6. Roll with (a.k.a. practically apply) sincerity by asking yourself, "Which decision will reflect my true nature?" the next time you find yourself at a crossroads.

# OFFERING: Prayer or Meditation

» So hum. = I am. Inhale "so," exhale "hum." Repeat.
» "I am safe."
» "I own my own bravery."

# Chapter 5

# EMPATHETIC

*"Letting someone know you understand the feeling he or she is experiencing is powerful, even if you can't say you have had the same experience. It's the empathy that counts."*

—M.J. Clark, *Shut Up and Lead*

## What Is the Essence of Empathy?

» Insightful, aware, mindful, and astute
» Patient
» Nonjudgmental
» Emotionally intelligent
» Kind and compassionate
» Just and impartial
» To imagine the feelings, thoughts, or perceptions of someone or something else outside yourself
» To have a sense of having a joint cause and connection with others

*"The most beautiful people we have known are those who have known defeat, known suffering, known struggle, known loss, and have found their way out of the depths. These persons have an appreciation, a sensitivity, and an understanding of life that fills them with compassion, gentleness, and a deep loving concern. Beautiful people do not just happen."*

—Elisabeth Kübler-Ross

## What Does Empathy in Action Look Like?

- » Accepting what *is* within ourselves and others
- » Listening to others
- » Practicing self-love, self-compassion, and self-kindness
- » Cultivating an awareness of yourself so that you can transpose that awareness and understanding to others
- » Being an active, thoughtful participant in the lives of others coupled with healthy boundaries for doing so
- » Recognizing we are more similar than different
- » Embracing our common humanity
- » Being in-tune with your relationships, the earth, and your own mind, body, and soul
- » Interacting with others in a thoughtful and giving manner
- » Encouraging others and communicating that you really care
- » Displaying a willingness to think outside of yourself and put yourself in others' "shoes"

*"Rejoice with those who rejoice; mourn with those who mourn."*
—Romans 12:15

## What Are the Obstacles of Empathy?

- » Shame or feelings of self-unworthiness
- » Judgment resulting from believing the lie of "perfection"
- » Sugar coating it for the other person
- » Giving credence to the lie of separation (of parts of ourselves, from others, and from our spiritual connection or God)
- » Trying to "fix" what's "broken"
- » Tuning out, checking out, numbing out

The Basic School (TBS) is the six-month small-unit leadership, infantry tactics, academic and physical training school that all newly commissioned second lieutenants in the United States Marine Corps must endure before they graduate to lead real Marines in the fleet. No matter whether you are destined to be a lawyer, pilot, logistics officers, or "grunt," or whether you are male or female, as a new Marine Officer, you spend six months of your life fully immersed in what feels like an extended boot camp.

During our twenty-mile hike at TBS, with more than a hundred pounds of gear on our backs, I remembered feeling so sorry for myself. I had two broken bones in my left foot, nerve damage in my left shoulder, an arthritic knee, and had just survived an aggressive bout with impetigo. No less painful, I was going through a divorce less than a year after getting married and suffering the emotional aftermath of the legal proceedings from reporting being raped by another service member. My platoon and company-mates used to jokingly say that TBS actually stood for "The Big Suck" or say it should really be called BOHICA, which stood for Bend Over Here It Comes Again. Point being, it was a time and place in our Marine Corps lives that no one enjoyed, even if you had no external drama going on in your life. I don't know of one Marine Corps Lieutenant who wasn't miserable at some point during TBS, if not throughout its entirety. Yet, I believed my six months there were harder than they were for most, given everything going on in my personal life and my smorgasbord of physical injuries.

*There's* no *way anyone else could be feeling worse than I am right now*, I thought on that suffocating, drizzly day, as my boots beat a rhythm on the road that wound through Chancellorsville Battleground. Our company of about 220 men and 12 women groaned and moved together like a digital-camouflaged human python. We must have been about fourteen miles or so into that final hike when I felt especially sorry for myself. Then, I called to mind something I had then recently read. I had just finished *Don't Sweat the Small Stuff* by Richard Carlson, PhD, and in that book was a reminder that I took to heart: to remind myself that I don't know what's going on for everyone else; I don't know their personal pains or their struggles. Maybe someone else was in more pain than I was, and it hit me that it didn't even matter if someone else *was* in more pain than I was or not. Pain is relative. But taking myself through the mental exercise of empathizing with others simply got my mind off the self-pity track and on one where I felt consideration, instead of contempt, toward others. Reviewing the *Don't Sweat the Small Stuff* chapter of "Develop Your Compassion" was something I did on a daily basis while at TBS

83

because I had to realize that my peers' pain was just as real to them as mine was to me, whether I thought mine was "worse" or not. Everyone has personal battles; I didn't own the market on struggles.

*"We must learn to regard people less in the light of what they do or omit to do, and more in the light of what they suffer."*

—Dietrich Bonhoeffer

Empathy hinges upon perspective and awareness. You cannot begin to feel or understand someone else's situation if you are always stuck inside your head or (inaccurately) believe you are the only one who has ever been through what you have been through. We must be aware of what is happening around us.

For instance, have you ever found yourself smack-dab in the middle of a swirling pool of self-pity, believing that you have had such a horrible day, then all of a sudden you find out one of your coworkers' children is in the hospital? Doesn't news like that put things into a different perspective? As often as we may feel like our pain or heartbreak is entirely unique to us, if we broaden our view just a bit, whether through personal experience or what we read in books, we find that the things that torment us are the very things that frustrate, wound, and stall everyone too.

As for awareness, I want to share a little story. I read it in Brendon Burchard's book, *The Charge,* and it is about a circus elephant that had been trained to be docile from an early age. He had to be because, well, he was a large animal and the trainers could not have him running around crushing people. So he was tied to a rope, and each time the elephant tried to walk away, the rope or his trainers restrained him. The elephant was physically restricted so often that he become mentally restrained, as well. Eventually, the elephant stopped even trying to walk away, at which point, the trainers removed the anchor end of the rope. The elephant was then no longer actually attached to anything; it just had a rope around its ankle. The elephant was free to walk away, but because he had been conditioned to believe he could not, he stayed put. He was un*aware* of his own freedom.

Can you identify with the rope around your ankle? Can you become conscious of its inability to hold you back, and step out and forward into your life instead? Once you have become *aware* of your personal rope, have you found it easier to identify that rope in others?

Do not zone out of life; remain present in your own life and for others and live it fully! Maybe you have been stuck at one point and wish you could realize that you were not actually tied up anymore, or you wish others would have empathized with your situation when you *were* actually "tied up?" Or perhaps you've been the one judging someone else for being stuck and held yourself above those mired in drama or trauma. Life is cyclical, what goes up will come back down and back up again. I encourage you to empathize with those who are down and out even when you are not because there may be a day when *you* need someone's compassion.

When you are feeling compassion and gratitude, it is impossible to get stuck on yourself. Your ego gets out of the way and you tap into your spirit without even having to think about it. Divine emotions are the best way to activate self-healing and repair toxic emotions, environments, relationships, and substances that have festered within your physical body. And thanks to the amazing body-mind connection, as you heal your body, in-turn you heal your mind.

Let's not think of "be more empathetic" as one more thing we have to add to our to-do list; rather, I encourage you to practice empathy with others as a reminder of your compassionate, generous, honest, and peaceful fundamental nature. Incorporate empathy into your lifestyle.

Where do we start though? With self-compassion. When we wrestle with the opposite end of the spectrum—self-criticism—things can get ugly fast. Our brains get pretty darn close to literally shutting down a bit as they go into protection mode against ourselves because when we are constantly self-critical, the body and brain react negatively to that, and we often end up abandoning what goals we may have to improve or grow. On the other hand, if we offer a self-compassionate perspective for ourselves with grace and patience, it turns on the security and care-giving parts of our brains. Thus, we end up at least having a shot at getting where we want to go. It might be uncomfortable getting "there"; transformation usually is. Transformation requires uncertainty (tempered by faith) and discomfort (coupled with compassion).

In the yogic tradition, the *yamas* and *niyamas* are the ten ethical precepts that allow us to be at peace with our families, our communities, and ourselves. This is big stuff, and I'm only going to scratch the surface on these concepts in the next few paragraphs. The *yamas* and *niyamas* comprise one of the "eight limbs of yoga," and tie-in closely to the type of empathy I describe in this chapter. Specifically, *ahimsa* (compassion for all living things) is the *yama* (wise characteristic) directly related to empathy.

Although *ahimsa* is typically simply translated as nonviolence, the principle goes much further than the basic premise of not killing others. First, we must learn how to be "nonviolent" with ourselves in the sense of embracing a gentler attitude versus our usual internal monologues riddled with destructive self-judgment. If we uttered these words to others, we would have no friends; yet we easily fill our own heads and hearts with self-inflicted negativity. This can be something as simple as denigrating our image when we look in the mirror in the morning, or deeper-seated beliefs about our self-worth. Negative internal monologues damage our capacity to be empathetic. If we are constantly berating ourselves, we stay stuck inside our heads locked away in self-pity, creating an environment in which it becomes impossible to sympathize with others. The sooner you stop repeating disparaging thoughts about yourself or pessimistic beliefs about your future or other people, the better. When we are so hard on ourselves all the time, it becomes nearly impossible to be understanding, forgiving, and nonjudgmental toward others.

Mature perspective, awareness of our own emotions, and being vulnerable play a part in insight, an insight that remaps our brains and gets us firing "on all cylinders," an insight that empowers us to feel for and identify with others. Moreover, as we continue to cultivate a gratitude practice, we increase the messengers from brain to body telling us "all is well." As we practice more gratitude, we build better health.

As we perpetuate negative thoughts, though, we harm our abilities to grow and live freely. Therefore, extending compassion to ourselves first, then to others, underlies the unity inherent in the energy of this world. It becomes nearly impossible to remain removed from the pain of others when we realize how much we are all connected. As we embrace this connectivity, we find ourselves wanting to reach out to and help others or cultivate a deeper respect for nature and our various environments. We realize that harming others harms ourselves. So it's a circle of self-compassion and empathy that rolls round and round!

The fall of 2008 was a time in my life when I learned the deeper lessons of empathy in an unexpected way . . .

"It will cost about $7,000 to save his life. What do you want to do?"

I looked at the dog. He was a Cocker Spaniel, but was mistaken for an Irish-Setter puppy during several of our walks. He had a name, but I did not think of him as "Bailey." He did not feel like *my dog* yet. In that moment, he was simply a financial liability with which I was now burdened.

*Really? Seven* thousand *dollars?* I thought. I lowered myself to the well-worn wooden benches of the veterinarian's office. My head dropped toward my chest as my body weight sank even deeper, forming a capital "C" made of flesh and bone. The smell of wet dog, cat pee, and unidentifiable feces dissipated as my consciousness cinematically faded out, and my memories took over . . .

*I need a morale boost*, I thought. *What better way to lift my spirits than to get a puppy?* Okay, so I was not a seven-year-old little girl anymore, but puppies make adults happy too, and I wanted one.

I had a list of logical reasons to justify my desire for a new pet and why that week was the week to make it happen. I had contemplated buying a "new" dog for over a year but had held off because of a pet I still had (but which my parents were keeping), my crazy work schedule, and a long-distance relationship I thought would soon require my relocation overseas.

My seventeen-year-old dog, Teddy, who was then living with my parents in Florida, was straddling a rickety fence between life and death. My parents bought golden blonde, well-bred Teddy when I was about eleven years old; initially, he was the "family dog." Dog, brother, and I spent years exploring the creeks and running routes and trails of northern Virginia. Teddy is even featured in several childhood soccer official team photos, sometimes donning a jersey loosely secured to his small frame. Teddy officially became "mine," though, when I took him to college with me. The Tedster was a main attraction at many of my house parties, went running with my military buddies and me, and even rode on the team bus down to Alabama from Virginia when our college soccer team traveled there for Nationals. After graduating, I brought him to friends' houses like he was just another pal hanging out with the crew. No one questioned it when I walked into their home with the little guy by my side.

Teddy and I were inseparable until I had to deploy, during which time my parents took care of him for me while I was away. While in Iraq, I often sat alone in my room with my back against the concrete, ash-covered wall, my legs dangling off the edge of the bed, too tired to remove the dust-covered leather and rubber boots, which felt like bricks from my feet. And I would pretend Teddy was there too. I envisioned him pressed to the side of my thigh, his fur against my camouflage. I would reach toward the outside of my right leg and pat the blanket; with my eyes closed, I imagined Teddy goldy-locks beneath my palm. I would open my eyes, knowing I'd find only thin air, and my open lids to release my tears. Of course I missed my family and friends, but we could write, e-mail, and sometimes talk on the phone. I had no way to communicate with Teddy. I could not wait to get home and see him again. But due to my busy schedule as a Marine Corps Officer, my mother insisted on keeping Teddy even after I returned from my two deployments to Iraq.

Post-deployment, I moved again, this time living in an apartment—alone. Although I had not had a dog nearby me for years, I still had to stop myself from throwing scraps from the table as I finished a meal. Every time I almost dropped a morsel to the floor, I would frown, realizing there was no dog there to lick the food off my fingers. But I had yet to purchase another dog because I felt like I would be cheating on Teddy to get a new buddy while he was still alive, even though Teddy did not live with me anymore. So, I repeatedly dismissed my desire for a "new" dog.

Additionally, I was engaged in an overseas relationship, one that was serious, and one that required me to move to Europe as soon as my military commitment was complete the next year. Moving abroad with a dog seemed like too much to handle, thus I held off on bringing a new canine life into mine.

However, after more than a year spent daydreaming about bringing a dog back into my life, in the course of a week, it became clear to me that it was time to act on that yearning. My work life hit a pinnacle of stress; nagging feelings of being "unwell" for many months resulted in mysterious blood work, which gifted me with a misdiagnosis of multiple myeloma; my romantic relationship abruptly and unexpectedly ended, thereby thwarting my plans to move to the Netherlands within the year; and segments of family drama imploded. All of my best friends lived at least a plane ride away. I had some distractions available, but ultimately, I just needed an authentic, compassionate companion in my life again. Therefore, with medical, familial, and relational turmoil all brewing, with my personal romance deceased, and Teddy nearly gone too, I decided that getting a puppy would be a well-deserved picker-upper.

I had already peeked at a few adoption websites over the course of a few weeks, so when I was truly ready to find my new puppy pal, I knew where to go. I had found an Alexandria Virginia-based Cocker Spaniel rescue group, Oldies But Goodies (OBG) and knew they were having an event at a PetSmart where I could meet potential candidates. I went to it, but none of the animals captivated me. I kept researching online until I was able to meet another dog from OBG who was housed at the very same vet we used to take Teddy to more than a decade before: Deepwood Veterinary Clinic in Centreville, Virginia.

The rescue group had labeled Bailey "not suitable for a home with children." The abusers at his former home were five children. I hesitated. I visited my sister, who had three kids, regularly. But he was so cute in his picture, and only nine months old, so he still had time to change. I decided to schedule a visit, during which he was not vicious, although he nipped me a few times during our initial interaction, but I discounted it as normal puppy behavior. He also never stopped moving—darting about and jumping on me—but again, I accounted for the puppy factor. He was energetic, underweight, and a little surly, but adorable and sweet in his own right, and I figured he would morph into a love-bug after hanging out with me for a little while. Ten minutes after driving away from Deepwood, I called a representative at OBG to tell her I wanted to buy the nine-month-old English Cocker Spaniel with an Irish Setter coat.

The first few days did not produce the results I expected. My new dog, Bailey, was aggressive with other dogs and even bit me multiple times. I never had a pet with behavior problems before; thus, after I signed on to be a foster mom while the adoption paperwork was finalized, I second-guessed my decision. Yet, Bailey was not *all* bad. Even in those first few days, he had his sweet moments, so I tried to endure what I assumed would be a temporary bad-behavior situation. I figured he probably just needed more exercise and attention with a healthy dose of patience.

Thus, on day four of being Bailey's temporary parent, on a classic, crisp Virginia fall day, I took a long lunch break so I could go home, let him out, and we could both enjoy the day. We walked through the woods behind my apartment, following the meandering creek tucked away there. We took our time, sniffing and looking around, and worked our way out of the woods back toward the main road of the residential area. Less than fifty yards from my apartment building, as we strolled along the sidewalk about to wrap up our afternoon jaunt, the day was ripped in two.

The nineteen-pound pup, walking three feet in front of me, pulled against the length of the royal blue extend-a-leash. I held the hard plastic base in my right hand, thumb hovering over the catch-or-release button like it was a trigger. I saw a U-Haul truck driving toward us, rolling forward at about thirty-five miles an hour. Bailey crouched low like a hunting cat. I glanced at him and laughed, amused by his stance. As he paused in a pre-pounce pose, I shortened the distance between us and was about to mash the button down to secure the leash at its current, shorter, length. But in the next instant, he lunged at the truck. Frame by frame, I watched, horrified, unable to press the leash trigger fast enough to stop the seemingly infinite extension of the tight rope as Bailey sailed off the sidewalk onto the asphalt. I scrambled, letting go of the plastic base of the leash, grasping at the string that burned me as it cut through the flesh of my palms. Right over left, right over left, right over left, I tried to pull him out of the path of the oncoming vehicle. The rope only gathered slack beneath my hands.

Bailey tumbled in the undercarriage of the truck like an old shoe in a washing machine. I screamed. The truck belched him out from underneath its metal belly. He was flung against the curb in front of me, thwacking against it like rain-soaked garbage. I stood with cement feet, seemingly unable to act.

Then, a sound that still visits me in nightmares, emanated from Bailey's writhing body. This sound flipped a valve, releasing a gush of

90

tears from my eyes. My chest rose and fell, shuddering from rapid, shallow breaths. He was on his back, barely moving, but creating a noise so painful I almost vomited. I could only manage to stare down at him. I repeated a mantra in my head: *Stabilize him; do not move him*. I dealt with it in human terms. I knew that one should not move people who have just endured back or neck injuries.

I am unsure how long I stood rooted to the sidewalk. Before the truck hit Bailey, he and I were the only ones around. However, after impact, an elderly woman came to my side. She wore matching fuchsia sweatpants and sweatshirt, and her sneakers matched her white hair. I could hear the brogue of her Scottish accent when she hunched toward me and said, "Pick him up, honey." She put her arm around me, guiding me to the apartment building's parking garage, Bailey limp in my arms and still whimpering that stomach-turning sound.

The woman got in the passenger seat of my car. I transferred Bailey to her lap, walked around my red VW GTI, found my place in the driver's side, and I drove to the veterinarian. My neighbor—I learned later that she lived in the same building as me—entered the vet's office with me. As I began detailing the events to the personnel behind the reception desk, she slipped out, unnoticed. I was distracted by the bad news bombarding my brain.

"It will cost about $7,000 to save his life. What do you want to do?"

The message physically pushed me back a step away from the counter. I had only owned this dog for four days, and I was offered the option of spending $7K on him because he had rambunctiously leapt in front of a truck? I felt guilty for being mad. Despite my anger, though, the anguish of seeing this poor animal in such pain meant that I pretty much never stopped crying throughout the whole ordeal.

I asked the vet personnel to provide other options. There weren't many. Other than shelling out thousands of dollars, my only choice was to leave Bailey there, walk away for good, and hope one of the vet techs would adopt him if he lived. The vets informed me that they would keep him alive overnight, but that was all they could promise. I wept at the thought of Bailey dying, which made me think of my Teddy on his deathbed, hundreds of miles away from me in Florida, and my cries turned into lurching sobs.

*If it was Teddy, I would pay double the $7K right now. But it is not Teddy. It is a new dog, difficult to handle, Bailey.*

I went home. I called my parents. I called friends. I cried.

The next morning, I called a representative at Oldies But Goodies (OBG). I told her what had taken place. She held an emergency board meeting, and the next day informed me that the members had decided that OBG would pay for Bailey's emergency surgery and that they could have it performed at a specific facility for a deep discount since they are a 501(3)C group. I immediately drove to the local veterinarian, picked Bailey up, and transferred him to the hospital in Springfield where they would conduct the operation.

I had already planned to provide Bailey whatever emotional and physical support I could as he prepared for and completed the suggested surgery, help him recover a little bit, but then give him back to OBG. After that, it would be the rescue organization's problem to figure out. I did not have the time, money, or emotional strength to deal with the situation.

The surgeon put the broken dog back together like Humpty Dumpty with metal plates and screws. Miraculously, there was no internal damage, so his pelvic fractures were the only thing in need of repair. Either way, he required several days' recovery at the hospital before I could take him home. I visited him once during that recovery time. I was ushered into a large, bright room with one wall comprised entirely of wire; I saw my dog immobilized inside one of the small cages. His back right leg glowed purple and blue. I tried to pet him, and he quasi-snapped at me. I implored the vet techs for help, but they made expressions that seemed to say, "We have already been dealing with his attitude. Don't ask us for help." I sighed. I took my cell phone out and shot a fifteen-second video in which he looked like he was going to bite me again. I frowned and said my good-byes.

The day I picked Bailey up to take him home, I had had a characteristic day: get up at 5:30 a.m. after tossing and turning all night, drive twenty miles to work, take my stiff joints for a pound on the Quantico pavement, shower and dress in five minutes or less, eat instant oatmeal at my desk and remain there for at least ten more hours before getting back in my car and battling traffic from doorstep to doorstep.

I arrived at the Springfield Animal hospital with a sigh. I collected my wounded and drugged-up animal, put him in my car, and drove him home. I decided to have him sleep in the extra bathroom on the other side of my apartment on account of his incessant crying.

I closed the door. I grumbled. I closed my bedroom door. I huffed and puffed. I played ambient music. I quivered with stress. I could *still* hear him crying. Around three in the morning, I lost it. I could not stand the whining anymore. I stormed across my family room, threw open the bathroom door, scooped Bailey up, and carried him to my car. I plopped the dog on the floor, and drove back to the hospital with inhibited vision, and a snot chain running from my nose, dripping off my chin. My puffy eyes, mucous-covered face, and PJ-clad get-up startled the attendant on duty when I burst forward to her desk with a crippled animal in my arms.

"I can't do this," I said. I was so sleep deprived it physically hurt. "I just picked him up this afternoon from surgery. I am his foster mom. I can't do this. I have a crazy job. I have to go to work in a few hours. I'm already exhausted. Take him back." I thrust him toward her like an offering.

The attendant surveyed me. She was silent.

Her nonresponse actually calmed me down. I found a seat on the bench behind me. Bailey rested on my lap, my arms cradled him. My spine had a deep curve as I sunk even lower into my seat. "I can't do this . . . right?"

I barely heard what the hospital employee said. Something about keeping him overnight, but the rescue group may not take him back. Charlie Brown's teacher voice blared in the fog around my head. All I know is it did not sound like a viable solution. I did not lift my gaze from the little red dog in my lap. My bottom lip forced itself outward as if the weight of my furrowed brow pushed it there. I let my mind run away with my thoughts for a moment. My eyes darted side to side in their lowered gaze, seeming to sweep the linoleum floor in front of me.

Then, as quickly as my eyes danced left to right, they stopped. Some intangible switch in my brain flipped. If I did not take this dog home tonight, who would? No one else would want to care for him; I needed to help him. As I visualized actually leaving him at the hospital, my stomach flipped. I was not an abandoner. I did not do it before, and

I would not do it tonight. I made a commitment I needed to keep. Plus, he was a helpless animal; he needed my help.

An energy filled my spirit, and a tide within me turned toward trust. *I can do this*, I thought, and I let go of something in that instant.

"Wait . . . I can do this," I then said aloud.

I stood up. I half stumbled toward the reception desk. "I can do this. I'm sorry. I'm just deliriously tired and stressed out. I'm sorry. I'll take him home." My words came out in mumbles. The girl may not have even known what I said, but I turned around and shuffled out the glass doors. More gingerly than before, I placed Bailey on the passenger side seat on a pile of towels. On the short drive home, I looked down and to my right. "I'm sorry, Bailey. It'll be okay." Bailey shifted his gaze from the window toward me. I smiled, feeling the made-for-TV-moment. Then, Bailey pooped in the car.

"What?!" My exclamation was half question, half laugh.

*Of course*, I thought. "Hold on, little buddy!" I pleaded.

I maneuvered the car to a gravel area off-road, near an intersection. In my pajamas, in the middle of the night, on the side of a dark road, I jumped out the driver's side door and ran to the other side of the vehicle. I lifted Bailey up from his poop-covered throne. Then he pooped some more—on me—as I tried to get him out of the car to finish his business.

"Oh . . . my . . . gosh!" I couldn't *not* laugh at the situation. I held him like a hot potato as I ran toward a patch of grass. By the time we got there, though, he was finished going to the bathroom. No more pooping to be done. He looked up at me from the grass like *I* was the ridiculous one.

I gave him another minute or so just to be sure, then gathered him up once more to put him back in the car and complete the drive home.

In the bathtub at home, I talked to him as I washed the feces off his fur.

"Well, Bailey, we've been through some crap together, haven't we?"

I dried him off, patted him on the head, and closed the bathroom door. I chuckled and shook my head as I plodded from one side of the apartment to the other and plopped into bed.

I was not always able to find the humor within the challenges immediately following Bailey's surgery though. What I had hoped would be a low-maintenance, happy-time, new companion turned into a massive, emotionally draining time commitment. Bailey could not function beyond whimpering, whining, and snapping his teeth at me when I tried to pick him up to take him outside. He could not even walk without assistance. Struggling to do so, I had to lean over him, supporting him with a makeshift towel-sling that elevated his hindquarters, and half crab-walk behind him just to get him "walking" outside to go to the bathroom. When I returned to my apartment, I glared down at him as I rubbed my sore lumbar. My body was broken from the years of Marine Corps beating it had taken. Herniated discs, arthritis, tendonitis from feet to neck—I had a physical problem nearly everywhere, and my spirit matched my body. I was in therapy again, talking to the counselor about the nightmares I was still having about stuff that had happened in the Corps, problems with my family, and my failed romantic relationships. I barely slept, I dreaded work, I had countless medical appointments all over the DC area to squeeze into my already jam-packed days, and now I had this stupid dog to take care of.

Days of "wait and see" in regards to his healing turned into weeks, comments of "Just give him back" did not cease, and my frustration with the situation—and the dog—built. He required an inordinate amount of care, could not run and play, and was not even well behaved. I was busting my tail to help this dog, and he did not seem to even *like* me. I knew I could not give him back to the rescue group now because no one else would want to take care of him either, but I fantasized about what my life would be like without him in it, allowing a sourness to fester within me.

On several occasions, even the audible expression of his pain was too much for me to handle. I jumped out of bed to stomp across the apartment, heave the bathroom door open, and scream at Bailey to "just shut up." Usually that was at two in the morning when I had gone to bed at midnight and had to get up for a job I liked, but in an environment I hated, around five the next morning. The yelling did not help—it never did—but I was too busy feeling sorry for myself to think logically, let alone give intensive care to an equally grumpy dog. He required wound care, medication, pills, shots, and attention and love I did not want to give at inconvenient times of the night.

I eventually felt badly about keeping Bailey in the other bathroom, though, and started to let him sleep in my room with me. One time, though, it was more than the sound of Bailey that got to me.

I rolled side to side in my bed, gradually awakening. I paused on my right side, then peeled my eyelids back just far enough to gain vision. I observed the glowing 3:00 on my digital clock. I let my lids drop. I relaxed on my back. I was not surprised to have my evening interrupted. I inhaled deeply, prepping for a woe-is-me-for-never-making-it-through-a-night-without-waking-up-at-least-once sigh. But my breath was halted halfway.

"Oh no."

For that brief instant before my mind stepped off the ledge from denial to acceptance, I wanted to believe that what I sensed was *not* what I sensed. "Please no." My eyes were still closed. I finished my inhale.

I reached toward my nightstand, turned the light on, and was bombarded by what lay before me. It was even worse than my nose led me to believe. My bedroom was covered. Not the solid kind of dog poop you can pick up, but the kind that looks like it started out solid on the first three expulsions, then morphed into a rancid fluid that is somewhere between barf and feces.

The expletives that flew out of my mouth in that moment would shock anyone. I catapulted myself out of bed. I became a human volcano. "Bailey!!!!!" I erupted with such force that he crawled under my bed, leaving a new trail of excrement behind him. I reached below the dust ruffle, grabbed him by what little scruff he had, pulled him out into the open, and screamed in his face. "Why!"

Something very tight within me came unwound. Thoughts that had nothing to do with Bailey ran through my mind: how tired I was, how lonely I was, how dissatisfied with my job I was, how much physical pain I was in, how sick I felt, how I pitied myself for the nightmares I still had about the rape and failed relationships and career goals. I kept spewing. "What is wrong with you! You stupid dog!" I wanted to hit him.

"Why, why, why, why, whyyyyyyyyyyyyyyyyyyyyyyyyyyyyyyyyy?!"

His body quaked. I hovered over him like a monster. I could *feel* the glazed-over look in my own eyes. I suddenly felt such a dark part of my spirit that its intensity brought me slamming back into the present moment, and I stopped the overflow. As quickly as the tremor started, it stopped, and my growling morphed into sobbing.

I wanted to throw up, not just from the smell of his crap and bile, but from the realization of the beast I had become.

"Oh my God, I'm so sorry, Bailey. I'm so sorry; I'm so sorry. It's okay."

His petite frame still shook. I lowered my torso toward him, pressing my forehead to his. I spoke quietly, apologizing, still crying.

When I left my bedroom to retrieve cleaning supplies from the kitchen, I discovered even more soupy brown and fluorescent yellow piles dotting the family room carpet. I clenched my fists, then released them. An hour and a half later, I was back in bed surrounded by a cloud of air freshener.

About a month later, Bailey regained functional strength and a situation that initially required daily, intensive care evolved more into biweekly physical therapy visits. When he could at least limp on his own without me lurching behind him supporting his back half, some tension between us started to dissipate. Although his shaved right leg and back still drew stares when I took him outside for bathroom breaks, our relationship felt more "normal." I found myself feeling honored to explain to gawkers that he had survived getting hit by a truck. When I told people the story, I swear Bailey listened to me. He would tilt his red head to one side and fix his eyes on me. He sensed my change in tone.

Generally speaking, Bailey seemed to be mellowing out more day by day. He snarled at other dogs less, and we smiled more on our brief walks outside. When we spent time together inside, he grew increasingly affectionate, snuggling in my lap while I read in the evenings, skillfully finding the perfect nook in my arm or leg in which to settle his white-capped chin. His budding warmth began to mellow *me* out. I talked about him more often and with less venom in my voice. Coworkers visited me at my cubicle to inquire about his well-being. Instead of becoming visibly stressed while giving a status update, I beamed as I relayed what new accomplishment Bailey had achieved that day: his healthy weight gain, improved endurance on walks, and "cuddle muffin" status.

I observed his idiosyncrasies not as annoyances, but as cute behaviors that only *my* dog performed. Clearly he was the only canine that assumed a military stance first thing in the morning, low crawling across the carpet as soon as he woke up, enjoying the sensation of a self-induced belly rub, right? Although many dogs have a "happy dance" to perform at the mere sound of the leash being lifted from its doorside hook, Bailey's series of whimpers, jumps, and turns were unique; he looked like a smaller, furrier fawn prancing in circles when I brought my hand to the doorknob. Unlike "normal" dogs, he almost never barked; instead, Bailey communicated in a particular sequence of squeaks with the intonation of human speech. Or what about the eye roll he sent my way when I said something I thought was hilarious, but Bailey thought was mundane? Did he really understand what I was saying?

We had tolerated one another's outbursts—his, the howling kind, mine the crying, sometimes vice versa. I was still just his foster mom, telling myself I would care for him until he was healthy enough to give to someone else, but I no longer festered over a situation I could not control, accepting it for what it was and trying to improve it if possible.

Then, six weeks after Bailey's surgery, as I left my top secret secured office to grab a quick coffee at the on-base Starbucks with my buddy, I checked my cell phone in my car. It was 9:30 a.m. I had a voicemail from my mom. "We are going to have Teddy put to sleep at 12:30 this afternoon."

"What?" I forced the word out through clenched teeth. My mom began her defense. I hung up on her. I called my father and unloaded on him. I had asked my parents to give me notice before Teddy was going to pass so I could get to their house and see him one last time. I boiled in pain. I called my mom back.

"You are not putting him down today. Keep him alive until I get there."

I still met my friend, Troy, for coffee. I told him about my parents' plan. "Sarah, fly to Florida. I'll take care of Bailey for you."

I drove back to work and explained the situation to my boss. Without hesitation, he said, "Don't worry about a thing here." That was my green light to go.

I bought a plane ticket, left work, packed, and drove Bailey to Troy's house. My buddy had a cocker spaniel too. In fact, he bought his dog from OBG after falling in love with Bailey, so he was happy to take care of my new dog while I tended to my old one.

98

I landed in Florida less than thirteen hours after my mom's call. I flew into an airport two hours away from my parents' home; they both made the long drive even though they had to get up early the next morning. When we connected at the airport, the three of us held our embrace uncharacteristically long. Nobody said a word. I opened the back right passenger door of their car to find Teddy on the floor, motionless. "What the hell? I thought they were going to keep him alive? They let him die anyway!" My head filled with lightning. I lost my breath, then checked for his. My palm found his ribs; it was easy to feel them through his thinning fur. They were moving, barely, but they were moving. Without lifting his head, he opened his eyes and looked right at me. I brought my forehead to his, and my tears soaked his fur. My hands now on either side of his face, finding those silken patches of fur on his cheeks; we stayed that way, in our own world, communicating in silence.

We began the voyage home. I murmured motivation to Teddy all the while. It was election Tuesday, and NPR correspondents discussed the results. Barack Obama had won. My father voted for Obama, my mother didn't, and their discussion was a distant din in my mind, as I never removed my gaze from my sweet boy at my feet.

Over the next three days, my mother and I, who were not often affectionate with one another, hugged each other and Teddy innumerable times, spent hours sitting together on the couch with our beloved between us, and told countless stories about The Ted Meister as if he were a person. Our seventeen-year-old dog's heart was half filled with a rare tumor and his lungs were full of fluid, but he had gained inexplicable strength during my visit.

His final appointment was still scheduled on the afternoon of my last full day in Florida.

"Do we really need to put him down? He seems so much better. He is eating again now."

My mom and I called the vet. I explained the turn in tide. The doctor assured us we still needed to bring him in as scheduled.

My dad left work early so we could all drive to the vet clinic together. Although barely able to, Teddy walked into the medical facility on this own accord. His blond hair was nearly white, and his ribs and S-curved spine were visible as he haltingly progressed forward, but he was dignified in his effort. I followed behind and to the left. I opened the door for him and let him enter the office. We entered the lobby. People looked up from their own loved ones to witness the procession of dog, daughter, mother, and father. As Teddy passed, they bowed their heads. My soundless weeping did not cease.

When our whole family filled the exam room, I questioned the vet in person. He explained that Teddy's turnaround was simply a matter of him "soldiering up," trying to be strong for me. That evaluation made me feel worse *and* better about the inescapable immediate future. My Teddy Ruxpin had gathered up every last bit of strength he had and more to show me his love, to say, "Mom, look at me, aren't I a good boy?" My love had breathed more life in him, as his had done for me. Teddy's kind spirit enhanced mine. My mom and I had not raised our voices at each other once during my entire visit.

But the inevitable arrived. The doctor and his assistant detailed the procedures to follow. Their words were muffled by my sniffling, by my swirling. Nothing moved in real time. The vet stood opposite us, arms hanging forward and hands clasped. My parents and I stood as a unit, intent focused on our blond baby as Teddy took his last breath. My mom and I were already in tears, but my father—and the vet—joined us when Teddy's chest stopped rising and falling with his life force. No words were uttered, but I heard the prayers of my parents as the pain registered in all of us. And we remained there, in the stillness.

When I flew back to Virginia the next day, the other Cocker Spaniel was the last thing I wanted to see. I was obligated, however, to retrieve him from my friend. Bailey did run to greet me when I arrived at my friend's apartment, but I only half-heartedly reached down to give him a pat on the head and usher him out the door with little fanfare. I felt like the emotional progress the red dog and I had made took two steps back. I had lost a piece of myself in Florida, and I transposed the pain of my loss—of Teddy, of my relationship, of my own health—onto Bailey. He seemed to be a manifestation of what was going wrong in my life.

I spent several days tending only to Bailey's basic needs. I walked him and fed him, but intentionally withheld affection. Unintentionally, I almost called him "Teddy" nearly a dozen times. Bailey handled the situation better than any person would though. He did not protest. He did not demand more. He was not overly energetic. He patiently waited me out as a more subdued and sweeter version of himself.

As life does, though, it went on, and at some imperceptible moment, like when boiling water turns to steam, my walls dissolved. Bailey had respected my pain; he let me grieve. And as broken as I felt, I knew I would heal; I knew I would love again.

Nearly four months after the accident, Bailey's fractures had healed, the pins and screws were removed, but a new problem had reared its ugly head—nerve damage. For four weeks, I took Bailey to the vet twice a week for physical therapy sessions. The therapist also gave me a brace to fasten to his back right paw, which essentially pulled the paw forward and flat, and a strap fastened to the upper part of his leg. Bailey would dance-walk with that bulky, black brace secured around his leg. His expression of pain and confusion was matched by mine imploring him for forgiveness. The brace did not seem to be helping, but I used it anyway. The times I didn't secure his gimp paw, he would run on it until it was raw and bleeding. As much as it displeased Bailey, I did not want to risk infection.

Even after all the physical therapy sessions I took Bailey to, and after trying different braces and various treatments, he still dragged his back right paw. This lingering injury was more external than internal: he did not let that numb paw slow him down. On visits to my friends' house in Maryland, Bailey would run and play with their German Shepherd-mix puppy and full-grown Labrador retriever mutt and have no qualms with keeping up with them. Bailey was increasingly lively as he gained strength through healing. After each physical therapy visit, though, the vet would bring up the topic of amputation, but then concede that sometimes normal function can return much later. Nerve damage is tricky. Would amputating this young dog's back right leg be the best option? What if he just needed more time, or more therapy? What if I somehow had Bailey's leg removed before it had completely healed?

I was still only his "foster mom;" I had not officially adopted him yet. With the exception of a couple of friends, most people continued to tell me to return Bailey to the rescue group. Logically, that alternative made sense. I had bought a dog to have as a hiking, running, and adventure companion. Now, though, with such a severe and permanent injury, he would be better suited as the lap dog of a sweet elderly person, right? He was running around now, but it wasn't really safe to let him do so, and if he lost his leg, that would surely slow him down.

Furthermore, I had to consider the cost. An amputation was another $7,000 surgery. I did not have that kind of money available and still had not made up mind on whether or not to fully adopt Bailey.

I had to consult the rescue group once again. They gave me two options: finalize my commitment to Bailey, and they would pay for the second surgery, or return him to OBG and have no more involvement with him whatsoever. I had three days to decide.

I prayed as well as sought the advice of my mentors. The next day, I contacted OBG to tell them I wanted to keep Bailey and that he needed to have his leg amputated. The surgery was scheduled two days later.

Post-op number two was emotionally charged in a different way than the first. My heart was fully committed to my companion this time. I had accidentally fallen in love with bratty Bailey, and so had my friends who had already helped me take care of him on multiple occasions. He had a very distinct personality that, with a little understanding on our part as humans, we saw as unique and amusing traits instead of annoying differences. I mulled this over during Bailey's surgery, and when the vet approached me in the waiting room after performing the operation, I tried to read her face. Her expression was somewhere between happy and sad. She almost looked confused.

"I saw something with Bailey today that I've never really seen before," she said. I could see a stack of wrinkles on her forehead. "The right leg was completely lifeless; all of the muscles were white and gray. It wasn't just a matter of nerve damage in the tip of the paw. Turns out his entire right leg was dead. Amputating ended up being the best decision after all."

I released the fist-like tightness in my belly. My upright spine relaxed downward as I exhaled a "thank you" to the doctor. Even though I felt confident to move forward with keeping Bailey and concurrently deciding to have his leg amputated, there was still a tiny part of me that was terrified that I would have ordered a premature amputation of a young dog's leg only to find out he just needed a little more time to heal. Even with that nagging fear setting up camp in the back of my mind, my heart had told me to move forward with the final surgery. And it turns out the spiritual and emotional guidance I received was spot on; I had followed my gut and now had results to offer relief. I slept well that night and looked forward to picking Bailey up the next day.

I retrieved my precious pup the following afternoon. I was bundled up when I entered the hospital, not only because it was February in Virginia, but to insulate myself from what I feared might be bad news. The vet techs commented on what a sweet animal Bailey was. I smiled close lipped, head bowed, thanking them for their heartfelt care. I drove us home from the vet, taking the turns well below the speed limit. Once there, although he weighed a mere twenty pounds, I side stepped through my doorway to make sure I did not accidentally knock Bailey into it. He was made of flesh and fur, but I treated him like crystal. Moving slowly, I knelt, with Bailey still cradled in my arms, toward the ground, eventually placing him atop his bed of blankets, which was now positioned adjacent to mine.

He rested on the left side of his body and tried to sleep. He remained very still, but wept human-like tears, moistening his fuzzy face, before finally falling asleep. I cried too. I believed that he would never look "normal" again. His entire back right hindquarter was shaved bald and the area of his missing hind leg looked as though a drunken person had stapled his gaping flesh back together along with some raw chicken skin. I mourned his loss for him, said another little prayer for his big heart, and tried to get some sleep myself.

Bailey slept through most of the next day. In the late afternoon when he awoke, I was not sure what to expect. I had stuck through it with this little guy, yes, but I had already resolved myself to the fact that he would never be the outdoor buddy I had originally wanted. So, to get ready for his walk, I fastened his blue collar around his glossy red, furry little neck, and took him outside to go potty. I carried him down the three steps that led out the back door of my apartment complex and set him upon the grass. I stood up. I stepped back. I watched him, waiting for him to make the next move. He hopped. I waited. He hopped again. Then, he began hopping so fast it became a run. Bailey's energy tugged at the leash. He was begging to run. We followed the wooded path we had walked the day of his accident, we beamed from our hearts, and we *ran.*

For months after the surgery, people stopped, stared, sometimes gasped or pointed, and asked questions. But I always walked him with my heart elevated, not because I was proud of myself but because I was overwhelming proud of my little trooper. Once the hair grew back over the bald spot, even the questions ceased, and for the most part, Bailey blended in with the pack.

As the winter months began to lift and pass, so did my pessimism. About the same time that Bailey seemed to be really filling out physically and emotionally, I reached a point where I felt I could discontinue my therapy, and soon thereafter I started dating someone. He lived in the same town as I did. He was mature, kind, and loyal; I was able to trust him. He understood some of the things I had been through. He was supportive of me and cared deeply for my Bailey.

This new boyfriend and I began to take Bailey on longer and longer runs. And even though that relationship ended later that year, a couple months after I left active duty Marine Corps, my healing did not halt. And my hey-let's-just-check-out-this-trail-type jogs I took Bailey on, often ended up turning into puppy-led, six-mile, single-track, all-terrain runs and swims. Bailey is not content to idly walk through the forest; he wants to *run*. He does not know he is a disabled doggie. When he runs, he is like a canine *Seabiscuit*—a little red runt, clueless that he is not supposed to be flying the way that he is, moving in such a way that the doctors claimed he never would again. He floats in pure bliss as he gallops, and I cannot help but grin from ear to ear when we sprint together. His joy is contagious. To see this three-legged Cocker Spaniel pulling as hard as he can at the leash, running as fast as he can over hilly trails, with what looks like an actual *smile* on his face, I am utterly inspired by the purity of his zest for life. The smile on his face always ends up on mine too.

Bailey is my teacher because he *lives* out the principles we all strive to. He and I were—still are—so broken. Yet, he is in the moment; he is happy; he is active and alive; and he has no concept of feeling sorry for himself. I do not take it for granted for one instant that he can move like that, that he is alive like that, that he is filled with joy like that.

My mornings start with gratitude because of Bailey. Even when I grimace to get out of bed, because I still struggle with a myriad of my own physical limitations, I always kneel next to my pup, lower my lips to his silken fur forehead, kiss him, and tell him, "I am thankful for you." When I am sick, he spends his day on the couch with me. On days I feel like I cannot accomplish anything, I look to him for motivation. On days I am sad, he is my shadow following me around the house and snuggling by my side. On days I feel sorry for myself, I remember Bailey does not feel sorry for himself, and I tell myself to get over whatever pity I may be feeling. Bailey is a living, breathing, moving example of all that I aspire to be as a person.

There comes a time in life when things become clear. You choose your path, and you walk it with the people—and the pets—who will walk it with you. You create your journey. You surround yourself with people who smile, who make you laugh, who are faithful, and who know when to wag with excitement and when to remain silent. Love those people who treat you right; love them passionately and without restraint. For those who treat you poorly, wish them well, but be willing to continue your walk without them. Life is too short to be anything but content with who you are, who you are with, and what you are doing. If you fall down, that is okay; tumbling, stumbling, and breaking is part of life. Get back up, regain your footing, and keep on running.

> *"There is no prescription for finding moments of gratitude in every day; there is simply the choice."*
>
> —Gillian Deacon

Deep down, as humans, *we just want to be known*—by others and by our God. Empathy really strikes at the core of that most basic human desire. Think of that in regards to the state of your own heart the next time you relate to someone else. Think about *knowing* them, even if for only a moment; be present, fully listen, and empathize with them in both the pain *and* the joy. Seek to understand before being understood and see how that shifts your relationships.

I admit, I do still find myself struggling to empathize with others in certain situations until I realize, in that moment of judgment, I have a choice to let my experience galvanize me against someone else or to empathize with them in understanding that every story is unique, and reasons for courses of actions are someone's own and do not reflect upon my own. In a way, it's a form of healthy depersonalization. It's never about us as much as we usually feel like it is.

Moreover, and what Bailey reminds me of too, is that we're all broken, and we are all more alike than we are different. Within our brokenness, we are one and beautiful and more Christlike than at any other time. Because in that brokenness, there is actually space for so much more. "There is a crack, a crack in everything. That's how the light gets in." My mom repeats Leonard Cohen's words to me often.

# Roll Call: Empathy

*"By reengaging people with their emotions, therapists help people find a greater sense of self-care and empathy for others."*
—Brendon Burchard, *The Charge*

1. Who are your empathy "roll" models? What about them do you admire?
2. Who are the empathetic people in your life? Describe a time someone was truly empathetic toward you.
3. What defines a happy and connected sense of empathy to you?
4. Describe a time you were truly empathetic, as well as a time that you weren't. How did the two instances feel different?
5. What would you have to do to improve and deepen the empathy of your relationship with yourself and with others?
6. In considering *ahimsa*, it's helpful to ask: are my thoughts, actions, and deeds fostering the growth and well-being of all beings? Ask yourself this now and see what you come up with. Do you need to make any changes?
7. Roll with empathy by being a great listener and mirror in conversation with statements like "I imagine you must be feeling . . ." Remember, take pause, be quiet, listen, and provide compassion and support for others.

# OFFERING: Prayer or Meditation

» "God give me the grace to be with my own pain, my own bravery, and my own joy, as well as with the pain, bravery, and joy of others."

» Or try putting empathy into practice via gratitude. How do we "feel" grace within ourselves? Being thankful for where we are right now can bring some forgiveness and positivity into our lives pretty darn quickly, equipping us with self-compassion that then fuels sustainable compassion toward others. As we feel better within ourselves, we are better equipped to offer understanding and patience to ourselves and others.

I think this meditation from Deepak Chopra and Oprah Winfrey is one potential way to do that:

"We will extend our understanding and experience of gratitude to the mind-body connection. Gratitude is much more than an attitude or mood; it is a powerful positive input to our mind-body system that leads to increased physical and psychological well-being.

"Grateful thoughts and meditative states don't just stay in your mind. Messenger molecules instantly transmit their effects to the body's 100 trillion cells, creating new brain cells and new pathways and brain patterns. The practice of gratitude has even been found to change our gene expression in a positive direction.

"By directing our awareness toward gratitude, our entire mind-body system is automatically oriented toward greater health and balance.

"Our centering thought for today is: Every thankful moment makes me healthier."

So, repeat, "Every thankful moment makes me healthier."

*"It is astonishing how elements that seem insoluable become soluable when someone listens, how confusions that seem irremediable turn into relatively clear flowing streams when one is heard. I have deeply appreciated the times that I have experienced this sensitive, empathic, concentrated listening."*
—Carl R. Rogers

# Chapter 6

# MOTIVATED

*"Motives are like the rudder of a boat. The motor moves the boat, but if the rudder is just slightly set at the wrong angle…well, you can end up in the wrong place."*

—John Blumberg

## What Is the Essence of Being Motivated?

- » A sense of deep purpose
- » Your cause
- » Steadfast direction
- » Mission, drive, passion
- » An inspirational attitude
- » A fundamental need or desire that causes you to take action
- » An aspiration driven by inspiration
- » An openness to creativity, novelty, surprise, and challenges to energize our drives

*"Ability is what you're capable of doing. Motivation determines what you do. Attitude determines how well you do it."*

—Lou Holtz

## What Does Motivation in Action Look Like?

- » Living, breathing, real-life displays of purpose-driven inspiration and action

» Embodying an accurate and authentic knowledge of your "why" and living in accordance with it
» Allowing your goals to be your guides
» Incorporating faith and trust into your drives
» Being a thriving example to others
» Serving your highest purpose and subsequently serving the well-being of everything and everyone else with whom you come into contact

*"Individuals can affect the world by becoming a model or an example in their small circle of influence. Just as a rock thrown into a pond causes ripples to gradually keep going out until eventually they are very small, so our acts influence the ecology of the entire human race."*

—Stephen Covey

Kate is one of my closest friends from our Marine Corps ROTC days, and I would frequently say we were "Moto Kitties" whenever we went out for an especially difficult, long, or fast run. "Moto" was short for motivated, and "kitties" was just because we were bouncy, cheery college students who cracked ourselves up with our own bad jokes. Usually, we did more than run though. Many mornings, as midshipmen at the University of Virginia, we would arise at 4:00 a.m.—about the time many of our peers were stumbling down Cable Avenue after a night at the bars and frat houses—load all of our gear into her forest green Mitsubishi Montero, and drive out to the woods to dart like maniacs over the river and through the woods with twenty, forty, or sixty pounds of gear strapped to our feminine frames. We would hurl ourselves over pull-up bars unnaturally placed between two trees, which we could barely reach, climb walls, slide ourselves along wire tight-ropes traversing murky streams, and crawl under barbed wire—all in the spirit of self-improvement, growth, and challenge.

We wanted to be the best.

We made ourselves as strong as possible, as smart as possible, as motivated as possible, not just for ourselves, but for the future Marines over which we would take charge when we became officers.

But what was driving us to do these things that 99.9 percent of other college students would never imagine doing? What inspired us? What drove us? Why did we do what we did?

We were driven by something bigger than ourselves. We were determined. Even as nineteen and twenty-one-year-old college coeds, Kate and I were hell-bent on doing everything possible to ensure we had a strong foundation before entering the metaphorical and literal battleground of the Marine Corps. We desired to become leaders who were well equipped to support and empower our future troops. As Marines and as women, we wanted to be able to stand on our own two feet. We did not want to allow anyone to be armed with the ammo to tear us down or to tell us we should not be Marines. We had dreamt of becoming leaders of Marines, and we weren't going to let anyone wake us up from that dream.

*"A dream becomes a goal when action is taken toward its achievement."*
—Bo Bennett

It was my all-encompassing mission to become a Marine. It was a goal I was so resolute to reach that I was willing to put everything in my nineteen-year-old existence on the line for it—physically, mentally, emotionally, and professionally.

Let me explain—the short version—but in a bit more detail.

When, after two years in the Air Force ROTC program, I began the process of making an unprecedented move and switch to Marine Corps ROTC, this decision incensed nearly every single person in my life, alienated me from my parents, and put my education on the line. I faced the possibility of thousands of dollars in penalties for breaching my scholarship contract. I attended the University of Virginia on a full ride from the Air Force. A scholarship cadet had never left or switched programs that late in the game. I was told it was impossible to do so. I had already begun my third year in college, and in order to cover all my bases had enrolled in Air Force, Navy, *and* Marine Corps ROTC coursework and leadership training. I was working a part-time job because I knew I would lose my scholarship, but kept playing club soccer and pursued my double major in sociology and religious studies. I never slept, but it did not matter. I was motivated by certainty. I knew with every fiber in my being that I was *called* to be a Marine.

Could I have justifiably employed the excuse that I was unable to follow my dream because my parents forbade it? Sure. Could I have said, "Well, I really wanted to be a Marine, but I would've gotten kicked out school, so I didn't do it"? Of course. (Although I didn't because I busted my butt to explore every option *other than* getting kicked out of school and had the grace and good fortune of working with people who wanted the best for me.) Could I have said financially it just wasn't feasible because even if they did let me stay in school, I would lose my ROTC scholarship and then have to pay my way through school? Well, yes, but instead, I did Navy/Marine Corps ROTC, Platoon Leaders Course, and got a job at a local country club golf shop to help pay my bills. I took action; I made it happen. Most of the time, I did it with enthusiasm. After a long fight, after many battles, I won the "war" and became a Marine.

> *"Everybody can be great because anybody can serve. You only need a heart full of grace, a soul generated by love."*
>
> —Martin Luther King, Jr.

What motivates me nowadays is a little different, but no less important. I do not want to push my body to the breaking point, I do not want to lead Marines (although I miss them like crazy), and I do not want to study warfare, tactics, and intelligence. However, I still do want to serve others. Subsequently, I am driven by a respect and deep gratitude for my spirit and body in learning how to heal it, because I want to be able to help others heal too. I want to lead students and young adults, and I want to be a life-long student of happiness, health, and meaningful success. One thing that remains a constant motivation is that sense of service. The mode of that service looks a little different now, but my servant spirit is the same as it was before, and helping others is where I find my greatest satisfaction. Serving others gets my mind off myself, allowing me to forget about my own tough situations as they arise, and gives my life a deeper purpose. Knowing that I may have inspired even one person to live their life with more passion, with more faith, and with more beauty keeps me rolling forward.

I wrote in earlier chapters about the continuity of my sense of motivation driven by service, as I do believe faith, service, sincerity, empathy, and motivation are inextricably linked. They feed and fuel one another time and time again.

Motivation is what spurs us on when we think we can't go any further. We become driven by a decision we make to either continue building our strengths or to change the things we don't like about ourselves, our situations, relationships, jobs, faith life, physical fitness, or health. We must be motivated to make ourselves and the world a better place. Here's a little secret: the happier you are, and the more you follow your dreams and live where you believe you should be living, then the better you, everyone else around you, and the world will be.

Winning is paramount in our society, but if you are going after the proverbial gold medal for all the wrong reasons—for the wrong motivation—then it is worthless. You have to know *why* you want to "win." If winning equals genuine, lasting success of a significant nature, then I say go for it. When we envision success what we are really longing for is the *feeling* we will have when we reach that defined point of accomplishment, right? The more sincere you are about what's driving you, the better able you will be to reach those physical, spiritual, career, and relationship goals and not worry about what anyone else around you is doing; the less likely you are to get sidetracked by comparing yourself to anyone else because you will be centered by your truest motivation.

Be guided through attitude, conviction, and commitment to take action, for action conquers fear! Are you afraid that you can't get the job you want? Go for it! Because, for example, is it really about the *job* or about *feeling* like you are providing a good life for your family? Are you scared you'll never lose those ten pounds? Be motivated to achieve deep, lasting health, not because you just want to look good but because you know it will improve your overall confidence. Are you unsure of your ability to maintain a healthy relationship? Do not allow fear to paralyze you; stop making excuses, educate yourself, and, as rapper Ludacris would say, "Roll out." Get out there and be vulnerable, be sincere, and have confidence because you want to be deeply satisfied in your relationships with everyone.

Without knowing your true, inner impetus for doing what you are doing, you will remain stuck forever where you don't want to be unless you let down some walls, invite inspiration in, and take action based on what fills your innermost drives, your heart, and your soul. Clarity through action!

*"Each time a person stands up for an ideal, or acts to improve the lot of others, or strikes out against injustice, he sends forth a tiny ripple of hope, and crossing each other from a million different centers of energy and daring, these ripples build a current that can sweep down the mightiest walls of oppression and resistance."*

—Robert F. Kennedy

## Roll Call: Motivation

*"Keep away from people who try to belittle your ambitions. Small people always do that, but the really great make you feel that you, too, can become great."*

—Mark Twain

1. Who are your motivation "roll" models? What about them do you admire?
2. Describe a time in your life when you lived out motivation. Also, describe a time in your life when you lacked motivation. What were some of the differences between those two times?
3. What defines happy and connected motivation to you?
4. What would you have to do to improve and deepen the motivation within your personal and professional relationships with yourself and with others?
5. God speaks to us everywhere if we only open our hearts long enough to listen. Will you be motivated by His whisper, His talking, or will you require Him to shout and shake you to your core before you follow your path? Imagine being told your time on earth is limited. What would motivate you then? Money, status, job title? Or something else? Love of family, spiritual peace, health, fitness, lasting happiness? Take a moment now

114

to pause and imagine what you would do with one year left on earth.

6. Roll with motivation by identifying your deepest why and letting it be your guiding light.

# OFFERING: Prayer or Meditation

» "I am strong."
» "God, comfort my heart, give me strength, and help me to carry on."
» Ask, and be quiet to receive the answer via meditation: "How can I be positive in my desires and purposely pursue them?"

# Chapter 7

# PERSEVERANT

*"Failure is the only opportunity to begin again more intelligently."*
—Henry Ford

## What Is the Essence of Perseverance?

» Committed
» Dedicated
» Disciplined
» Consistent
» Strong, courageous, and gritty
» Steadfast
» Passionate

*"Out of clutter, find simplicity. From discord, find harmony. In the middle of difficulty lies opportunity."*
—Albert Einstein

## What Does Perseverance in Action Look Like?

» Pursuit of your goals and devotion to stay the course
» Adherence to your path no matter what bumps in the road you encounter along the way
» Doggedness in making the contribution to yourself and to others that you were meant to make

» Striving to turn obstacles into opportunities and tragedies into triumphs
» Refusing to live with a victim mentality and choosing to live with a victor mind-set
» Diligence in the pursuit of the personal, professional, spiritual, and health ambitions of what you believe to be true, worthy, and admirable
» Hopes and dreams infused with a resolute spirit
» Living, leading, and loving by example

As we segue from the Motivated chapter to the Perseverant chapter, I am reminded of Brené Brown's explanation of the difference between guilt and shame. To paraphrase, she says that when someone feels guilty, it has the potential to be a helpful motivator because the person essentially realizes they made a mistake and they have the potential to correct or improve it in the future; they see the behavior as separate from who they are as a person. Shame, on the other hand, results when someone feels that because of something they didn't do right or well, that they are a bad person.

I think shame often arises, too, when we get into that vicious hamster wheel of comparing ourselves to others. In my experience, I am more than willing to work hard, own my mistakes, and strive for excellence (not perfection), and can feel pretty good about that whole process even when the going gets tough. Where I get dark with myself fast, though, is when the motivation for my perseverance is driven by insecurity, jealousy, or pettiness resulting from comparing myself to someone else. I end up feeling ashamed of myself, and my motivation can die on the vine in a hot second.

In those instances, I do my best to remind myself of three things:

1. I cannot compare my middle to someone else's end. Like John Wooden says, "Never try to be better than someone else. But never stop working to become your best self."
2. I don't know their story. They don't know mine. (Yup, even when it's someone I actually know! I don't really know what it took for them to "get there," good, bad, or anything in between.)

3.   Additionally, perseverance is not something to be discussed; it must be *lived*, demonstrated, and . . . wait for it . . . *practiced!* Perseverance absolutely can be an intentional, mindful practice that cultivates a daily discipline within us. Although conceptually understanding it and making a verbal commitment is a starting point, we must then display, eat, live, breathe, and *perform* perseverance in order for it to be a real thing.

*"You can only go halfway into the darkest forest; then you're coming out the other side."*

—Chinese Proverb

About halfway through my first deployment, I stumbled across the opportunity to try out for the All-Armed-Forces Women's Soccer Team and, with my Command's approval, planned to do it. First, I would have to try out for the All-Navy team. Then, if I made it, I'd compete against the other final teams from all the other armed services in another tournament. After that competition, an all-star team would be chosen to compete at the Conseil International du Sport Militaire (CISM) level in the Women's World Cup. By April of 2006, though, when I returned from my first deployment to Iraq, chubby from chow-hall food and stressed out from 24/7 work, I wasn't exactly prepared to compete at a high level of sport. I hadn't touched a ball in about five years, I was insecure about my soccer skills, and I was battling early signs of a stress injury. I was very intimidated by the whole concept of it all because unknowns tend to be scary, but I knew it was a very honorable thing to even be selected to try out. I wasn't sure if I was good enough, but I still wanted to go for it.

Everything was going well, and then a couple weeks into training, I pulled my right quad and found out that the excruciating pain I had in my left foot was from osteoarthritis. Had I been an excellent player at the time, I could have shifted to my nondominant foot without too much trouble, but c'mon, at this point, I was only playing at an average level with my *dominant* foot. Without much of a choice, I tried to compete with my left foot. I made it through the remainder of training by taking it easy but still practicing. Then, before I knew it, it was time for the Army and Air Force teams to come to Florida for the tournament.

I knew I wasn't prepared athletically or physically and felt additional frustration due to some stress with my then-boyfriend who had also just returned from a deployment. We were both dealing with standard elements of post-deployment stress, and I was not sleeping well at night. I was fatigued and feeling a bit psychologically delicate.

The entire evolution was emotionally charged. This all-star team meant a lot to me because I thought it could be my second chance to be a "real" soccer player. I'd given it up in college but thought, *Wow, maybe I can do it now!* Unfortunately, the tournament did not go well.

There was an awards banquet at the end of the tournament whereby the All-Armed-Forces CISM Team was chosen. My dad was there, like the old days, supporting me, watching the games, and even attending the banquet with me. They announced the team and I wasn't selected. I cried after the banquet as I explained to my father all the things I should've done differently. I'd put my whole heart into this, but when it boiled down to it, I just wasn't good enough to make the final cut.

In situations like that, it's easy to think of excuses—and I did. At the same time, I also took responsibility in knowing, point-blank, that my skillset just wasn't there. I was as upset as I was because I thought that was going to be my only chance at making that CISM team. I left Florida believing I would never get that soccer opportunity again, and that August, I returned to Iraq.

However, the next year I ended up being able to make it to the tryouts for the new team! The coaching staff was different, there were no separate service teams, and the camp was shorter in duration. All the servicewomen who were trying out had to show up for one trial camp where people were cut one-by-one over the course of a couple weeks until the final team was chosen. Within the first few days, the coach told me I was a definite qualifier. Then a recent Naval Academy grad and a West Point grad showed up late to the camp. They were quality players, and as a player who was there from day one, it was difficult to see them show up and seem to be getting preference; it was an uncomfortable situation for the players who had been there from the get-go. Furthermore, by that stage in the camp, my quality of play apparently went retrograde, and instead of knowing for sure I would make the team, I was on the cusp. The arrival of new players, combined with my waning performance, resulted in the coach downgrading my status throughout the camp. By the end of training, he told me he wasn't sure if I was even going to make the final cut. But that wasn't all . . .

Another big factor was the tenuous social dynamic; the team was split into two groups. I felt like I was in middle school, but *worse*! (Hello, adult bullying!) The mean-girls dynamic was extremely difficult to deal with because it wasn't just personal; one group's dislike for the other was reflected on the field insofar as picking teams from only their close friends or only passing the ball to each other. Perhaps they thought it was funny. To the rest of us, it was juvenile and hurtful, not to mention, demoralizing.

At the end of the trial camp, the coach informed me I was an alternate. As a team, we had a five-month break between the tryouts and then regrouping to train for a couple weeks again before our Military Olympics competition in India. During that break, I got a call from the coach almost every week; every conversation held a different conclusion. I was an alternate. I was on the team. I was an alternate. I was on the team. I had no idea what to prepare for later in the year! Was I going to play or not? On top of it, I was trying to decide whether or not to stay in the Marine Corps since my initial four-year commitment was up, and my stress injuries were ever-present in my daily life.

By the time fall 2007 rolled around, I had already decided to stay in the Marines another two years and had moved from California to Virginia. The coach's final call, a few weeks before the training camp start date, brought good news: "You're going to come back. You're the 18th person on the team." Since we only carried eighteen on the roster, it was his way of saying I was the lowest man on the totem pole, but I'd made it! I planned to return to the team with a great attitude and to work my butt off. I didn't care if it felt like half the girls hated me; I wasn't going to give them any extra ammo to dislike me due to my work ethic or attitude. I vowed to be positive because I was so grateful for what felt like a second chance.

Fast forward to India: I did not play one minute of one game. Externally, I smiled as much as possible and cheered on all of my teammates; internally, I felt worthless. I didn't think I was the best player on the team, but I felt like I was at least good enough to be given a shot.

Even in the last game—a friendly match against Canada—the coach told me to warm up because I was going to play, then never put me in. Add that to the incessant, inexplicable animosity from the players in the "clique," and soccer-wise, 2007 was a really tough year. But I tried to make the most of it. I had fun, socially, while I was in India and made some life-long new friends.

As the 2008 tryout date neared, I began to see 2007's experience in a less critical light. I was playing more soccer again and my skills, not just my fitness, had improved. Therefore, I felt more confident about the soccer part, even if I was still unsure of the social aspect. I thought, *I should just go back and have the best attitude possible. I'll kill them with kindness and prove my salt on the field.*

Only a couple of weeks before the 2008 trial camp, my boyfriend broke up with me. It wouldn't have been such a big deal except that I was definitely still struggling with some elements of post-deployment stress and depression—frankly, I was not mentally healthy. I was glad I'd stayed in, but the job I had at Quantico was high pressure with a lot of responsibility. As most jobs in the Marines involve, I was pulling long hours, and fatigue magnified any emotion—high or low—that I felt.

So with the added stress of a sudden breakup, I wasn't handling things well. I knew I was in a fragile emotional state and didn't want to go to soccer and deal with petty people. It wasn't an unknown anymore; it was a known, and I didn't want to deal with the "mean girl" dynamic. I really had to take a step back to evaluate the situation. I prayed about it. I knew I loved soccer and I knew I could choose to have a good attitude if I put my mind to it. I also knew I'd been playing more frequently and improving my soccer skills. So I decided, "How about I suck it up and prove that I am strong mentally and physically?"

That year, I had more friends on the team and started off on a strong foot both playing-wise and socially. With new girls on the team, ones who I could mentor, I got my mind off myself. I stepped more into a service mind-set with my focus on guiding the newer members of the team through some of the rough waters they experienced. Getting my mind off myself gave me the attitude adjustment that I needed. Even though I wasn't an officially sanctioned team captain, I still had a leadership role to encourage the younger and/or newer players and comfort them when they felt bullied, as I had being the new kid the year before.

The 2008 CISM World Cup was held in the Netherlands. That time, I started every game and played every minute. And it felt awesome! It was restorative to my soccer core to know that I came back and I had earned a top spot on the team. I had doubted, prayed, and felt like God had given me a kick in the butt (along with encouragement and support from other people) to get back out there and try again. There was still mean girl drama that year, but it wasn't as severe as the year before.

At the tournament's close, I went back home to Northern Virginia. I played intramural soccer all summer and fall, and the majority of spring in 2009 until it was time to go back for that year's tryouts. Once again, I prayed about it beforehand and hoped for less drama since it seemed to decrease year by year; even so, I felt like I had to mentally prepare each time before leaving for the trial camp because anything could happen there.

My last year on active duty in the Marine Corps was 2009, and the soccer experience that year would essentially be the capstone to my military career. The timing of the camp and the tournament was such that as soon as I got back to my current Marine Corps job at the end of June, once soccer was over, I would only have a week or two left, then I'd go on terminal leave. My bosses were very supportive of my membership on the soccer team, cheerleading for me to go and do well, so all signs pointed in a positive direction.

I went to Mississippi where the tournament was being held that year, and as soon as the final team was chosen, the coach announced the team captains. I was one of two. I was thrilled! I was proud of myself for coming back year after year, learning to rely on my faith, on my friends, and on my own hard work. A few days later, I wore the blue-and-white striped "captain" armband with pride, stood in the center circle, and watched the referee toss a coin into the air for our first game of the tournament.

As odd as it may seem, my soccer experiences closely paralleled what had happened in my Marine Corps career during those same years. In both arenas, the 2006/2007 timeframe was an arduous one. I basically hit a low point—feeling like my Marine Corps career wasn't going in the direction I envisioned. I faced some big setbacks in my professional and personal life. Relationship after relationship seemed to crash and burn. Yet, by staying in the Marine Corps another couple of years I'd progressed past some stumbling blocks. By the spring and summer of 2009, I had come out on top in both soccer and my career. I was in a completely different place than I had been in 2007. Seeing it all come together in 2009 gave me a sense of faith and promise about things. I'd followed devotion, intuition, friendship, and mentorship down a path I could be proud of. I kept chipping away at things year after year even when it seemed hopeless or even when family and many friends told me I was nuts for going back again (both in regards to soccer and the Marine Corps). From the outside looking in it didn't make sense for me to stay in the Marines or to go back to soccer, but I did because something within me told me, "Go back." Thank God I did, and thank God for those people who were positive influences who encouraged me to do so. Because there I was in the summer of 2009, at the pinnacle, and I didn't take it for granted for one second.

By April of 2010, after a mission trip to the Turkish Republic of Northern Cyprus, some international volunteer work, and general globetrotting, I was ready to reintegrate into the "real world." My declaration that "I'll know when I know" when it was time for me return home had materialized: I knew. My intuition let me know that I was done with traveling for the time being and wanted to start working again. I got a job with a DOD contractor in Northern Virginia and Washington DC. I found a great niche with a small, personal company. I counted myself fortunate to find something unique among the conglomerate of intelligence contractors in the area. The company that hired me was composed of down-to-earth, laid-back people who were equally competent and personable, with bosses who wanted me to combine my social science and intelligence backgrounds. It was ideal.

Not long after I began my new job, I confirmed that I would be able to play soccer again that year as a reservist. It felt like an exciting time. Within those last few years, I had become an established player on the team. Getting to play again in 2010, reunite with soccer girlfriends, and travel to France for the CISM tournament was a mixed bag again in many respects, but overall a positive experience. In seeing my own continuity and perseverance, though, I put 2011 in my sights as the ultimate goal: I would turn thirty that summer (age goal), it was the next Military Olympic Games (performance goal), and it was going to be held in Brazil (travel goal). I was still living in Northern Virginia, working full time and not traveling constantly, so I was able to condition, again, with Gaelic football and lots of soccer. The tryouts for the team, which would compete in the World Games in July of 2011, had to be held in March in order to allow time for people to get their visas well in advance of the competition.

However, once March rolled around, I wasn't at my peak performance. The assistant coach commented that I looked fit but was weaker and getting knocked off the ball more than usual. Basically, I didn't look as strong. I was somewhat disappointed in my performance—I'd made the team but wasn't what I considered to be a high-quality player. Therefore, I was determined to return for the pre-Olympics training camp in July tougher and better in order to display to my teammates and coaches that I should be there. I was committed to turning that potential obstacle into something that would drive me to grow.

Thankfully, an opportunity for growth presented itself. In May of 2011, I moved to Ohio and it was there that I picked up a new (and awesome) sport: Australian Rules football. "Aussie rules" gave me the new breadth of aggressiveness I needed. This quirky and rough sport brought me back into the fold of a regular and supportive team, as well as put me in the environment to get bounced across the field by a teammate and to pick myself back up again. The couple of months I got to practice and play with the Columbus Jackaroos (the men's team) and Jillaroos (the women's team) filled the void in my game to where, when the soccer team reconvened in July, I'd rebuilt my strength and was still lean and fit. It was rewarding to see my hard work had come to fruition again, and my confidence was reflected on the field.

We, Team USA, trained together in Florida for ten days before going to Brazil for the big show. The team was getting along well. I had a good feeling about 2011. Furthermore, I loved our assistant coach's style of training: lots of technical drills, organized practices, and constructive criticism. On the other hand, we still had the always-positive figure in our head coach. At long last, the coach and player dynamic finally felt balanced and healthy. Moreover, for the first time in soccer history, I wasn't dealing with any major life stressors at the time of the tournament! As I got further and further away from my deployment years and my active duty Marine Corps years, my personal life and mental state evolved into something much healthier—and it was reflected in my soccer. In that same vein of healthiness, I experienced something else new that year: focus. It, too, showed on the field.

Our team believed we had a real chance at success in the Military Olympics that year. Every year since 2007, we seemed to improve a little bit, and in 2011 we had the best group of girls and team dynamic. But for whatever combination of reasons and factors, that great feeling didn't equate with actual winning. We lost to Germany in our first match of the tournament. This was a loss over which I was slightly heartbroken because I knew that as short as the tournament was, that losing one game—the first game—would basically knock us out of any real championship contention.

Later that evening, we were out at the social club they'd set up in our Athletes' Village. I had a beer with my teammates and some of the other US athletes, and on the walk back to our building, our head coach summoned me. "Hey Sarah, come here!"

I walked over, and he lured me in with a simple question. "If you could get feedback from the coach of any country in the world, which country would you pick?" When I told him Brazil, his reply stopped every other thought I could've possibly had in that moment.

"The head coach of Brazil approached us after the game today, knew you by name, and said you were one of the best players on our team. He said you were good enough to play on the Brazilian squad." Excuse me. Did the world just stop turning?

"What?"

He repeated himself.

In that suspension of time, my mouth dropped open, I cocked my head to one side like a confused puppy, and I furrowed my brow. With a "hmmm" upon my face, I just stayed there for a moment. I let the release wash over me. In the span of a few seconds, where it's not mentally possible to think a million thoughts, a million thoughts is what raced through my mind. Full circle—*flash, bang* . . . hard work . . . *zing* . . . don't give up . . . a chuckle . . . thank God . . . a broad smile . . . Then my brain stopped, and it all came to a head in the instant of one comment. In a moment, it was real. Perseverance had, in fact, paid.

Like Winston Churchill said, "If you're going through hell, keep going." I felt as though I had gone through "hell" to make the team in the first place, returned year after year despite peer belittlement, and achieved a sense of it all coming full circle. Even before receiving confirmation from my coach that my hard work had paid off, I was grateful and glad that I had been tenacious. Rio was just the icing on the cake.

> *"I've been absolutely terrified every moment of my life—and I've never let it keep me from doing a single thing I wanted to do."*
> —Georgia O'Keeffe

I believe perseverance and motivation are closely tied because both require courage. In order to persevere we must be motivated by something compelling. Also, we must keep in mind that we cannot do it alone. Moving forward in the right direction, not just movement for a movement's sake, requires support, coaches, gurus, and mentors to guide us with answers and insights that empower us and ask us questions that enable us to tap into our intuition.

Perseverance is the means to your purpose because you will not let anything stand in your way in order to do what you know is right or accomplish what you have set your heart on completing. Likewise, we must intuit when to fight and when to recuperate by balancing perseverance and purpose with patience. Do not beat yourself up with self-defeating comments because you don't have it all figured out yet. Push forward and as author, and one of my beloved mentors, Daniel Allen often tells me, do as you *can*, not as you *can't*.

> *"Being confident of this, that he who began a good work in you will carry it on to completion until the day of Christ Jesus."*
> —Philippians 1:6

We simply must make up our minds not to be deterred by obstacles— imagined or real! It is a matter of perspective on whether we see barriers as obstacles that will stop us or as opportunities that will catapult us to growth. *The Chinese symbols for crisis and opportunity are the same!*

Moreover, we must accept that progressing does not require the perfect set of circumstances. For instance, in the Marines we were taught the value of the 80 percent solution. Although applied to battlefield situations, this lesson is easily transferrable to other areas of life: it will never be the "perfect" time to decide, you will never have "all" the information at hand, or you may never be exactly "ready" to do what you need to do, but you must eventually *do*. Sometimes, you only have 80 percent of the information, or less, required to make the "right" decision. Fixating on perfection and requiring it in order to move forward does not serve you or those with whom you relate, work with, help, or inspire. Your impact on the world needs to be made, and it doesn't have to be perfect to be powerful.

Purpose and grit are required; grit without purpose is useless. The two go hand in hand and their interlocking fingers form perseverance. Working hard without a tenacious and meaningful "why" will only leave you empty. Hard work is not valuable in and of itself; it must have a purpose fueling its perseverance fires.

Final thought: grit without grace can be exhausting. Remember to rest too. Be gentle with yourself when gentleness is called for. Restoration, time to recharge, and giving yourself the emotional and physical space to be present with and really feel what's going on for you provides a foundation for moving forward from a place of stability and strength.

> *"If you can't fly then run, if you can't run then walk, if you can't walk then crawl, but whatever you do you have to keep moving forward."*
> —Martin Luther King, Jr.

## Roll Call: Perseverant

> *"To learn strong faith is to endure great trials. I have learned my faith by standing firm amid severe testings."*
> —Charles Mueller

1. Who is a perseverant "roll model" in your life?
2. Describe a time in your life in which you were perseverant. Also, think of a time when you let your perseverance wane. How did the two times feel or look different?

3.  What defines happy and connected perseverance to you?

4.  Conduct a perseverance roll call by taking a "strengths inventory." List all your social connections or supports (family, friends, church, sports, school, work, etc.), practices (yoga, reading, prayer, etc.), physical strengths, emotional strengths, and mentors (role models, teachers, guides, etc.). These are the traits, the things, and the people who will help you build and sustainably maintain your perseverance.

5.  Roll with perseverance by: staying on your true path, keeping the big picture in mind, reminding yourself the worth of your goals, and striving to be your best despite the inevitable obstacles that arise to thwart you.

# OFFERING: Prayer or Meditation

»  "May grace dissolve the obstacles in my way. May I find strength where I thought there was none. May I find gratitude in the struggle. May I be supported by the people in my life."

»  "I am supported. I am loved. I am love." Repeat.

# Chapter 8

# ENGAGED AND EXCITED

Have you ever found yourself in the "flow" of things? Engrossed in a project so intently that you forgot to eat? Listening to someone's story with such focus that you lost track of time? Or can you remember a time as a young child when you seemingly never tired and could play for hours upon hours until your parents shouted for you to come home? "Engaged and Excited" is the "flow" part of *Just Roll With It!* Flow comes from connection to others, connection to deeper parts of ourselves, connection to Spirit, or a combination of all three of those. Flow can be felt emotionally, cognitively, or spiritually. It's a way of creating a new reality through unabated focus and fervor and is often an intense experience. There is a oneness that happens, a phenomenon of merging with your craft, or intimately connecting with another or with God. The better connected we are, the more engaged and present we are, the better able we are to be fully alive and excited about whomever we are with or whatever endeavor we are pursuing. Engagement has the capacity to fuel our excited fires!

> *"Enthusiasm is one of the most powerful engines of success. When you do a thing, do it with all your might. Put your whole soul into it. Stamp it with your own personality. Be active, be energetic, be enthusiastic and faithful, and you will accomplish your object. Nothing great was ever achieved without enthusiasm."*
>
> —Ralph Waldo Emerson

## What Is the Essence of Engagement?

» Fully present, not mired down by the past or obsessed with or worried about the future
» Connected, tied-in
» Interacting with meaning
» Not allowing distractions to detract from the interaction in which you are partaking
» Mobilized by the great energy within you through challenge and a requirement to utilize skill of some sort, which often breeds a spirit of creativity

## What Does Engagement in Action Look Like?

» Allowing yourself to be fully expressed, generating your own positive energy
» Generating creative works
» Connecting on a deeper level with others, fostering community, and building lasting and significant relationships
» Seeking out mentorship from those "above" you as well as reaching out to help those "below" you
» Stretching your own concept of self and improving your skills, beliefs, and physical and mental acuity by placing a greater demand on yourself or your environment
» Action that challenges you and brings focus and fulfillment

*"The purpose in life is to be happy."*

—Dalai Lama

## What Is the Essence of Excitement?

» Stimulated, stirred, energized
» Delight and pleasure in the activity in which you are engaged
» Love and appreciation
» Enthusiasm
» Energy
» Eagerness, passion, and zest for all that life has to offer

# What Does Excitement in Action Look Like?

Living in a spirit of enthusiasm and gratitude in which you anticipate what lies before you and what lies ahead with interest, curiosity, and eagerness.

Having an attitude based on a knowing that God has created this beautiful world for us, the landscapes for our journeys, our greatest fears and greatest triumphs. Let's roll in it, enjoy it, breathe it in, and be stoked that we are here!

> *"Alike and ever alike we are on all continents in need of love, food, clothing, work, speech, worship, sleep, games, dancing, fun. From tropics to arctics humanity lives with these needs so alike, so inexorably alike."*
>
> —Carl Sandburg

The need for us to stay engaged with one another and connected in excited, positive fashion is about more than just feeling good. Connection and social support impact our health on every level. Dr. Kate Hendricks Thomas is a health researcher who writes about the fairly personal way she came to understand the importance of social cohesion. In *Brave, Strong, and True: The Modern Warrior's Battle for Balance*, she writes about being crippled with shame after a messy divorce and domestic violence. Her inability to share the struggle with others stemmed from a fear of letting anyone see that she was imperfect.

This barrier to connection exists for all of us. What if we just admitted we are flawed, failing, and so far from perfect it is not even funny?

Social connection impacts our mental health, our emotional regulation, and our actual physical bodies. We are wired to connect with God and with one another, remember?

> *"Life must be lived as play."*
>
> —Plato

I started playing soccer when I was four years old, I began swimming competitively when I was five, added basketball at eight, horseback riding as well as track and field at nine, and as an adult, picked up a myriad of adventure sports like mountain biking, white-water rafting, hiking,

133

sky diving, snowboarding, wake boarding, surfing, and rock climbing. In 2009, I was introduced to one of my now all-time favorite activities: Gaelic football. And in 2011, I discovered something even stranger: Australian Rules football.

Okay, so what the heck is Gaelic football? It is a mix between soccer, basketball, volleyball, and rugby. Yup, leave it to the Irish to come up with something *that* whacky! But all jokes aside, I want to tell you a little bit about the role this sport has played in my life—it kept me connected during a time I was at risk of drifting away.

I know that to many outside observers, sports seem like simple diversions, fitness, and entertainment. But sports, especially team sports, have meant so much more to me than simply serving as a means to get exercise or build confidence. Maintaining participation in new sports, and challenging myself physically and mentally to build skillsets, has absolutely kept me both engaged and excited about life, true. Moreover, though, it has kept me connected to others in the community.

When I was in the military and played on the women's soccer team, even with all its drama, it kept me connected in a healthy way. It gave me a social outlet beyond the Marines. Since I left active duty, other adult-team sports have served the same purpose—a healthy, social outlet, connection, and challenge. Since 2009, every time I've moved, sports have provided an anchor point for me. For instance, when I returned to the DC area after my first big chunk of world travel, although I didn't have a job or much else in the way of stability, I had a team to turn to for healthy outdoor activity and social interaction when I was invited to join the Gaelic football team. It was as much a social club as it was a football one. Then, when I moved to Ohio, and found that they didn't have a Gaelic football team, thanks to my husband's investigatory efforts, I discovered another new sport—Australian Rules football—and I instantly had a huge group of kind new friends in a brand-new town.

I get that sports aren't for everyone, but find your "football" wherever you go. There are so many teams, clubs, service groups, Meet Up groups, and social organizations today that there is absolutely no reason not to go out there and get involved.

One of the best ways to weather any storm is to rely on others; find anchors in your friends and family, and if God hasn't provided you with those friends and family, you go out and find them. We cannot do it alone. We need teammates, mentors, coaches, and leaders in our lives. Even if we do have it all together, so to speak, we still need someone to keep us on track and guide us. My teammates and coaches have provided that for me throughout my childhood. As adults, most of us neglect that need, but we shouldn't! Adults need coaches too! Perhaps even more so because other than work, what source of mentorship or leadership do most of us have?

Dr. Kate Hendricks Thomas shares a story in her book, *Brave, Strong, and True*, about some research that perfectly illustrates the power of connection—of engagement—to build resilience. Kate says,

> A story I often share with my students is a hard one to hear for those of us who are animal lovers, but it paints vividly the concept of resilience cultivation. In this noteworthy demonstration endeavor, researchers used baby chickens to make the point that resilience is something we can learn through experience.
>
> Painting the chicks and grouping them in separate pens, the first group was left alone to interact happily and normally. The second group was periodically picked up and stressed in a confined space. After the stress, the chick was given time back in their group pen to recuperate. The third group was continually stressed in the confined space, with no recovery time or play opportunity with other chickens. The researchers created three distinct populations with different experiences.
>
> After raising them for a time in this manner, all the painted chicks were placed in buckets of water, with researchers timing their struggle until drowning. *I know, this sounds just awful.* It doesn't have a happy ending but there is an interesting lesson, I promise.
>
> The chicks that had been continually stressed drowned almost immediately; they had no hope in the face of hardship that they could swim. The second group to succumb was comprised of those "happy innocents" in group one who had never been confined and stressed. They didn't know how to withstand this watery hardship and folded in the face of it.

135

The last swimmers fighting to make it were the chicks from the stress adaptation group. Somehow, the confinement stressors followed by time to recover had rendered them stronger and able to swim and survive much longer than their peers. This group was resilient; they had experienced hardship before and believed they had a chance to make it and recover. They had those past mastery experiences to rely on, and they just fought to keep swimming.

Researchers interested in psychological and social determinants of health picked up the concept of resilience and have gradually extended its use from the domain of mental health to health in general. Early work on resilience was concerned with the individual, but more recently researchers have become interested in resilience as a feature of whole communities. Resilient traits can be taught, but this does not happen in a vacuum.

Although it's a terrible story about drowning baby chicks, this is good news! This means resilience is learnable, and one of the biggest ways in which it is, is through connection with others. Activate your engaged and excited muscle by combining several of the properties already discussed: choose fulfilling challenges that demand a singularity of focus, stretch your efforts and capabilities, strive for progress (not perfection), allow yourself to achieve a sense of completion, create an environment in which to share your experience and achievements. Focus on the journey not the destination and find joy in the process.

So here's the final scoop on this whole "Engaged and Excited" chapter. Get into the flow thing. Meaningful team, organization, social, and personal connections require vulnerability, and vulnerability requires relinquishing control, a façade of perfectionism, and sometimes, even some underlying shame, all of which requires being secure in yourself. Vulnerability is scary. I hear you. It, too, can be practiced though. Start in small, manageable chunks of vulnerability.

See how all these SEMPER traits are interconnected? Yet most of us are so terrified of being vulnerable that we never allow ourselves to fully engage—fully *connect*—with others, and to be completely excited about how we are living our lives. We keep walls up to keep people out and our excitement down. To what end though? What purpose does that really serve? You have "protected" yourself, but you also prevent yourself from experiencing the full realm of emotion and spirit that life has to offer.

It might seem a little silly, but I get so amped up for all my sports activities and I'm a grown woman! I get to travel and compete, connect and work hard, relax and have fun. What a gift that keeps on giving because it really does keep me engaged and excited about life!

A truly fulfilled life is about seeking out the things that keep you linked-in, challenge and enliven you, and bring you joy. This does not mean a hedonistic, self-absorbed pursuit of pleasure but rather a foundational desire to connect to your true essence and to others. And, frankly, there comes a time in life when things become clear. You choose your path, and you walk it with the people who will walk it with you, and you worry less about those who won't walk with you. You create your journey. You surround yourself with people who smile, who make you laugh, who are faithful, and who know when to burst with excitement and when to remain silent. Love those people who treat you right; love them passionately and without restraint. For those who treat you poorly, wish them well. Be willing to continue your walk without them. Life is too short to be anything but content with who you are, who you are with, and what you are doing. If you fall down, that is okay! Tumbling, stumbling, and breaking are all a part of life. Get back up, regain your footing, and keep on running. Follow the trail you have blazed, and discover that your true *living* is in the *journey*.

Keep that "strengths inventory" in mind from the perseverance chapter. Those connections are the cornerstones of your health and wellness, and are required elements of engagement and excitement, which build resilience.

Exercise your power of choice, make a decision, take action, put your heart into it, and lighten up. Think and *be* happy! Find enjoyment in life! If you're too busy feeling sorry for yourself, you'll miss all the good stuff going on around you. Chill out! Everyone is so stressed about everything all the time. Get freaking excited about life! Feed your soul by pursuing your passions and placing importance on relationships, and you'll be more fulfilled, focused, happy, and excited about everything in life.

There have been so many occasions where I could have justifiably "checked out" of life. Believe me, I get it if you're feeling that way. But I promise you, life is worth more than surviving; it is worth *thriving*. The quality of our lives is so much more than the ticking away of minutes on a clock or days on a calendar. So, go forward with zest, deep connections, and utter excitement about the gift that *is* this life; be a thriving example to others.

The SEMPER guidelines I have for living an engaged, excited, purpose-driven life are:

1. Keep it simple. "Live, love, laugh, leave a legacy." Stephen R. Covey.

2. In order to be excited, to be happy, to be enthusiastic, you really have to embrace the power of now. The more present you are, the easier it is to go with the flow and be happy and excited about what you're doing. The easier, too, it is to connect with others. However, if you are bogged down by worry about the future or weighed down by the past, you cannot enjoy where you are.

3. Laugh as much as possible. In fact, I challenge you to make it your goal is to be so excited about life so frequently that you break out into spontaneous laughter throughout the day. Besides the fact that it's fun and just feels good. "Laughter is also one of the greatest meditations. When you laugh, compulsive thought disappears, and you're completely in the present moment." Steve Ross, *Happy Yoga*.

4. Believe this truth: "Our birth right is happiness. We don't find it by attaining things. We're all seeking to find more happiness and suffer less." Rod Stryker

5. Allow yourself to be open to the unexpected and excited about surprises; living without expectation and attachment means you will be constantly growing, evolving, and changing. As you engage with others, it will be very exciting.

6. Be a lifelong student, a consumer of knowledge, and a seeker of evolution. Take heart that learning and practicing these character traits is a process that requires practice. "Learning is

not a product of schooling but the lifelong attempt to acquire it." Albert Einstein

7. Accept that freedom means making mistakes, and don't be deterred to take the bull by the horns because you're worried about imperfection. "Freedom is not worth having if it does not include the freedom to make mistakes." Mahatma Gandhi

8. Find the silver lining. Dark is required to appreciate the light. "Optimism is brightest when surrounded by the darkness." John Jacobs, founder of Life Is Good®

9. Get some fresh air and get movin'! Serotonin can significantly lighten your mood and promote a sense of happiness and well-being, and it is affected by the amount of oxygen you inhale. Fresh air will leave you feeling more refreshed and relaxed.

10. To paraphrase Brendon Burchard, one of the most successful entrepreneurs of our time and an all-around good person, life becomes mundane when you make it so, charged when you make it so. The power plant doesn't have power; it generates power. This underscores the power of choice; choose to generate your own power, enthusiasm, and energy. The people with whom you surround yourself obviously also play a huge part in this, as well, so take into serious consideration with whom you engage in personal, professional, and intimate relationships. Cultivate a discerning heart so you surround yourself with people who build you up, challenge you, and support and encourage you to grow. The value of teams, for instance, is being able to surround yourself with people who are stronger and faster than you are so you are challenged to stretch your boundaries and grow.

11. Pursue your passions! Do not settle for mediocrity; it will be the death of you. "There is no passion to be found in settling for a life that is less than the one you are capable of living." Nelson Mandela

12. Quite simply, I see the living out of "be engaged and excited" as being *happy*. I love this list of "12 Things Happy People Do Differently" from Jacob Sokol: express gratitude, cultivate optimism, avoid overthinking and social comparison, practice

acts of kindness, nurture social relationships, develop strategies for coping, learn to forgive, increase flow experiences, savor life's joys, commit to your goals, practice spirituality, and take care of your body. Sound like a few things that I have written about already?

13. Be patient. "Be patient toward all that is unsolved in your heart and try to love the questions themselves . . . Live the questions now. Perhaps you will gradually, without noticing it, live along some distant day into the answer." Ranier Maria Rilke

14. Embrace the flow!

*"People who follow their joy discover a depth of creativity and talent that inspires the world."*

—Robert Holden

Go for it already! Live that ridiculously happy life of your dreams. You got this! When you choose to make it yours, nothing can stop you. Sometimes we make it more complicated than it needs to be. God, other people, our friends and family, don't want perfect; they want present. Can we make "Heaven happen now" in our own authentic way? Something happening in us now means being engaged, being present, and as Matthew 5:3 illustrates, the kingdom of heaven is PRESENT. "Blessed are the poor in spirit, for theirs is the kingdom of heaven." Get 'er done spirituality—thinking that God will be impressed and help you—doesn't work. We need more "I got no game" spirituality, as we can be vulnerable before others and our God.

Keep it simple! Laugh, lighten up, be grateful, and *choose* to get moving in a positive direction!

# Roll Call: Engaged and Excited

*"Every thought is a seed. If you plant crab apples, don't count on harvesting golden delicious."*

—Bill Meyer

1. Who are your engaged and excited "roll" models? What about them do you admire?

2. What defines happy and connected engagement to you?

3. What would you have to do to improve and deepen the engagement and excitement you have with people and in regards to your life purpose?

4. Who is the most excited or engaging person you know? Do you ever find yourself thinking, *I wish I was more like her/him?* If so, what is preventing you from being happier or relating with others better?

5. Do you find that excitement and connection is contagious? Describe a time you've experienced this sensation.

6. What do you think about most often? Is it something that excites you, makes you smile, laugh, feel connected to others, or become positively energized? Or is it something that inhibits your ability to move forward?

7. Is there an activity that you used to do that you loved, that absolutely lit you up, but which you no longer do? Or is there a relationship from which you've disengaged that used to bring joy? If so, why? Is there a way you can reengage those connections and feelings?

8. Roll with being engaged and excited about life by refusing to live it any other way than to the fullest!

# OFFERING: Prayer or Meditation

» "I play. I create. I succeed."

» "I am connected. I am whole."

» What are you grateful for right now, in this present moment? Make a list. Meditate upon those items or offer prayers of thanksgiving for them.

# Chapter 9

# RESILIENT

*"The most beautiful people we have known are those who have known defeat, known suffering, known struggle, known loss, and have found their way out of the depths. These persons have an appreciation, a sensitivity, and an understanding of life that fills them with compassion, gentleness, and a deep loving concern. Beautiful people do not just happen."*

—Elizabeth Kübler-Ross

## What Is the Essence of Resiliency?

» The ability to return to your true state after being bent, broken, stretched, twisted, or crushed
» Strength factors outweighing risk factors
» Overcoming adversity
» Adaptability
» Recovery and rebirth
» Flexibility, strength, and balance in harmony
» Buoyancy in attitude and action

*"Holding onto anger is like holding on to a hot coal with the intent of throwing it at someone else; you are the one who gets burned."*

—Buddha

# What Does Resilience in Action Look Like?

» Behaving as someone who appreciates life and intends to thrive despite difficulties

» Spiritual, relational, physical, and nutritional health, for without health, resiliency is impossible

» Rising from the ashes—after being knocked down ten times, getting back up on eleven

» Embracing your sense of agency and power even within the smallest of choices

» Choosing to be optimistic versus pessimistic; putting your heart into it, lightening up, and thinking and *being* happy

» Giving yourself a chance to rest, recover, and reemerge stronger than before

*"If it doesn't challenge you, it doesn't change you."*

—Fred Devito

**\*Warning\***

Survivors of sexual assault will want to carefully consider whether to read this chapter. In it, I detail and contextualize the experience of being raped by a fellow Marine. I also discuss the anguishing politics of reporting rape. The result is a story meant to be illustrative and meaningful, but it does contain elements of violence.

"Hey, man!" I greeted my friend as he walked through the front door of my apartment.

"Let's watch *The Best of Chris Farley* tape," I said over my shoulder as he followed me to the living room.

He sat on the couch. I squatted in front of the VCR, thumbing through my tape collection before tilting the video forward and removing it from its case. I chuckled in anticipation of the unsophisticated humor about to bombard us from my TV. The post-party, SNL-viewing-while-chatting-about-life, ROTC, and work outs was a regular occurrence for us.

I hit play, then plopped down on the sofa next to my buddy.

Then, it began. I don't recall any transition from normal interaction to the barrage that assailed all of my senses. Instantly (it seemed), my dear friend was on top of me, then inside of me. Visualizing it now, like a removed third party, watching a tape significantly less entertaining than the comedic one rolling while this happened, it seemed like an eternity passed before my paralysis-confusion ceased.[1] In the maybe five seconds it took for me to neurologically process the attack I was under, I felt like my head had been forcefully, violently, deliberately pushed under murky water.

When I resurfaced, I screamed.

"No . . . no . . . NO!" erupted from me.

I screamed and gasped and yelled and shoved him off of me. Like a cartoon character dashing to and fro, thought bubbles formed above me, *This way? That way?* I scrambled to find my clothes while I yelled, "What the hell!"

"I'm sorry, calm down, it's all my fault, it's my fault." He tried to pacify me.

I bundled my pants under my arm and climbed my wooden stairs, hoping I'd be safe on the second floor, trying to get to higher ground. I ran to my room and slammed the door behind me.

I was in the fetal position, rocking myself, murmuring a mantra of "What the hell? What the hell? What the hell?" My surroundings were blurry, my thoughts a fog.

And there he was again. He had come into my room and climbed onto my bed. He sat next to me and put his hand on his shoulder.

"I'm sorry, Sarah. I'm sorry."

I couldn't think straight. I was crying so hard my gut ached. "What the hell, man? What the hell is wrong with you?" I wept into my open palms, pressing the heels of my hands into my cheekbones, giving my eyes room to breathe under cupped palms when everything else about me felt like I was suffocating.

His hand on my shoulder and apologies transmuted into more deliberate touches and then "I'm sorry . . . I know it's wrong, but I can't help myself." He got on top of me and began to grind himself against me, repeating his guilty declarations in my ear.

I screamed his name followed by a grisly "NO!" As confused as I was by what was happening, thank God I was awake enough at that point to ignite my defense mode.

In retrospect, this segment of the rape is what disgusts me the most. He articulated his wrongdoing then openly declared he would do it again (had I not defended myself). I feel sick to even write about it now, ten years later.

I threw fists at him in a fury and pushed him off of me. My hands were like a broom of fire as I forcefully, violently ushered him out of my room. I kicked, shoved, punched, and corralled him toward the stairs and pushed him down them. I followed behind and continued my own onslaught to ensure he was out of my home before shutting the door as quickly as possible and dead bolting it behind him.

Immediately after kicking my friend-turned-assailant down my stairs, screaming, flailing, throwing punches, and shoving him out the door, I called my then-fiancé, David, but he was asleep and didn't answer. (An occurrence he'd incessantly guilt himself over for years to come).

I needed to talk to *someone*, so I called one of my close friends at the time, Laura. My words came lurching out in puffs and spurts, along with tears and snot, and I gulped for what certainly wasn't enough air to form the words I needed. I told her what had happened, not leaving out a single, horrific detail. I couched it in terms of shame, telling her, "I'm not sure what happened."

"Sarah, you were raped."

But I was confused.

When I heard tales of rape, I used to think, *Why are all these rape cases so convoluted? Either the guy or girl said yes, or he or she didn't. Black and white. End of story.*

I had trouble envisioning an attack as being anything other than black and white.

I know now, with statistical significance to back it up, rapes are overwhelming committed by someone the victim knows. Which means—news flash—it's hardly ever "black and white."

As Senator Gillibrand said in the 2013 Senate Armed Services Committee Hearings about military sexual violence, the reason why these cases need to be removed from the victims' or perpetrators' direct chain of command is because commanders can't distinguish between a slap on the butt and a rape.

In the legal proceedings that later followed, neither could *my* commanders—both the one in my chain of command and those out of it. "It" all got lumped together as a couple of drunk college kids getting too touchy with one another; it was a matter of "he said–she said" that could never be resolved.

Kissing, touching, and hugging, is not penetration, however, and a kiss, flirting, or jokes do not warrant, welcome, or otherwise condone RAPE.

Rape is an act of violence; it is not about sex.

So, the fact that it was a close friend—yes someone I'd dated very briefly over a year before, but who really felt more like a brother than a friend to me—made it all the more unfathomable, all the more earth shattering, and all the more core rocking to the depths of my soul. I had defended this very guy when he had been accused of disciplinary and personal problems earlier that semester. I had said, "He's a good guy. Give him a chance," of course never knowing that grace would be turned against me.

The fact that it was a fellow Marine Corps Officer in training made it seem *unreal*. We were training to embody "honor, courage, and commitment." How could this happen?

The next morning, David's phone calls awoke me. I'd left him several messages immediately after the attack, as well as after talking to my girlfriend, but that morning, while he listened from Pensacola, Florida, and I sobbed from Charlottesville, Virginia, I painted the gory picture for him. His shock mirrored mine.

My friend who raped me also called me that morning. He apologized again and asked if he could call my fiancé and apologize. My fiancé agreed to take the call, noting that would be the last time he would ever speak to my rapist again.[2]

Later that day, I sought counsel from another close friend of mine, a male friend who was a fellow Marine classmate. After revealing the basic details of the evening, I made excuses, saying it was my screw up, that I should have reacted faster, should have stopped it, something, anything. Doubt simmered within the tone of my explanations though.

My words were like toes in the water to see how my friend would react. My statements sounded more like questions.

*I had been attacked in my own home by someone I loved. How would I ever make sense of that?*

He nodded as my self-blame rolled out, affirming my uncertainty.

But then I took a deep breath and said, "I hate to say this, but I *think* it . . . could've actually been . . ." and whispered the word, "*rape.*"

His reply still echoes in my mind today.

"Sarah, c'mon, that's not rape," he said. "Rape is when you're tackled in a dark alley by a stranger who forces himself on you."

I felt like I was in an afterschool special. I didn't know how I should respond.

However, this wasn't a made-for-TV special, it was my life, and I was in disbelief. As naïve as my own perceptions were about rape, even *I* knew that was a bogus comment. He loved me as a friend, was an educated young adult, yet even *he* didn't get it. I wasn't mad at him though—not then and not now. Even though the facts show that rapes are overwhelmingly committed by friends or family members, which only adds to the confusion and depression surrounding such an event, people still have the stranger stereotype in their minds.

A couple days after the attack, I went to my Marine Officer Instructor (MOI)—the major who served as the leader of the Marine Corps-bound students within the Navy ROTC Battalion—and told him I didn't want to be a Marine anymore. I told him that I'd seen some things recently that made me believe I couldn't, shouldn't, and no longer wanted to be associated with the Marines.

I intended on telling my MOI that day that I had been raped. I didn't though because it felt like I had been raped by my brother and had to tell my father what had happened. I did not even have the words to articulate it to myself, let alone a man I admired as much as I admired that major. I was ashamed of myself. If I told him the truth, surely he would judge me, wouldn't he? How could anyone believe such a heinous thing was even possible?

I hear from other rape victims all too frequently that their fear of reporting mirrored my own.

So, I didn't tell him what happened. I spoke in generalities about doubt.

And he was speechless.

Less than two years before, as partially described in earlier chapters, I'd put everything in my twenty-year-old existence on the line in order to pursue the calling to be a Marine. Physically, mentally, emotionally, and spiritually I had bull-whipped myself toward growth and success. Having grown up in a military family of Honor Roll student and Varsity athlete siblings, I defined myself by academic and physical performance.

I had transformed in those two years. I went from holding "unbeliever" religious status to being a new Christian and having the courage to follow God wherever He led me.

But that day, there I sat, concave, in front of a man I revered, announcing to him that I was about to abandon my calling.

The Major was poised behind his ship-like mahogany desk; I sat in an old-school leather straight-back wooden chair with brass nail head trim around the edges. It was one of those chairs that made you sweat no matter your mood. Half a dozen times in our conversation, I paused, about to say something more about what had happened, to tell him a fellow midshipman had done something to me I couldn't yet articulate . . . but I didn't. Instead, I wept and told him I faced the deepest doubt yet about my path.

I don't remember exactly what he said to me that afternoon, two weeks away from my commissioning—the pinnacle of my young adult life. Somehow, he convinced me to see it through. Maybe he thought it was just a particularly bad case of self-doubt I faced that week. As midshipmen, we were often knocking on his office door with the desire to vent our self-doubt about being Corps-worthy. We would leave feeling reassured without feeling patronized. He had a gift.

My mom likes to share what she's read, often saving newspaper clippings of passages deemed worthy of rereading or ones that adeptly express an opinion she held or describe a matter she considers important. She mails them to me wherever I live or holds on to them until she sees me in person.

Years later, my mom snipped and saved *this* piece, from Chapel Hill's *The News and Observer:*

A 2010 study commissioned by the DOD found about 70–80% of victims [of sexual abuse or assault] do not report their attacks. Soldiers remain silent because they fear that they will not be believed or that they will be blamed for sending mixed messages. They worry about being branded as weak or damaged or untrustworthy. Among the few victims who come forward, even fewer press charges.

With the thin paper resting in my hands, I closed my eyes and briefly drifted back to the time immediately following my rape . . .

I know why women do not want to tell, because before *it* happens to you, you never think that it *could* happen to you—a strong, self-sufficient person like you, and in my case, a Marine. This sort of *thing*, I preferred not to name it at first, only happened to unfortunate idiots—not that any woman ever "asks for it"—just that they must've been *not smart* in some way for *that* to happen to them. Of course, I thought *that thing* was horrible for people who truly were victims, but I knew with certainty it would not and could not ever happen to me. RAPE.

Therefore, when "it" did happen to me one week after getting engaged and two weeks before graduation, my natural conclusion immediately afterward was that it was *my* fault. Somehow it was easier to blame myself, punish myself, and commit to knowing I needed to change something about myself than to say I'd been sexually assaulted, let alone *raped*. I was a successful go-getter, so this was merely a mistake that needed correcting. I'd been drinking that evening, so it must have been a simple case of alcohol-induced, judgment impairment. Thus, I imposed a quick fix—I resolved to cut back on drinking and turn up the heat on my self-discipline regimen.

Days passed. But something still *hung* there. I ruminated over the night, the sequence of events, looking for clues as to how it could have even happened, where I stumbled, where I could place more concrete culpability on myself and move forward under that pretense of self-blame. The memories of that night rolled through my head like a movie reel of a tide coming in. I was the character suspended in front of myself.

Other than once whispering the word as a question to my friend, I didn't even call it "rape" for weeks after it happened because that word wasn't in my vocabulary with respect to myself. It was an unknown quantity, like cancer, that only happened to other people. I felt bad for those people for their apparent stroke of bad luck because I saw rape as a basic misfortune, as something that could be prevented if certain steps were followed.

In what would have been the normal whirlwind of events of matriculation, I went on with my life in a hurry—I finished finals, graduated from college, then got commissioned. From the outside looking in, there were no noticeable hiccups to my life's course of events.

One major exception to the calm façade occurred the night before my graduation. My parents, both of my sisters, my brother, my grandmother, David, and Laura had traveled from far and wide to witness my college graduation. The event was filled with requisite family stress. Then we went out for a few (what were supposed to be) celebratory drinks and by the time David and I got back home around two in the morning, I was hanging on by an unraveling mental thread. The creeping crack I had kept in check throughout the day violently ripped open like a fault line. Thanks to stress, fatigue, and alcohol, my spiraling thoughts got the better of me. I went down the rabbit hole, and in the comfort of my own home, now laced with violence, the flesh and blood of my soul earthquaked out. I kicked my bedroom door off the hinges. I screamed, cried, moaned, and yelled incoherencies. I slurred words, explaining the rape over and over again to my fiancé until I eventually collapsed in his arms.

I didn't sleep a single minute that night. The next morning, David and I packed my car and the U-Haul full of all of my belongings, waded through a day of graduation must-do's, then started my drive south to leave college life in Virginia and begin adult life in Georgia and Florida. I sucked it up. I swallowed the rape and let it fester inside of me.

For about four months I bobbed along the timeline of my life like a bottle tossed to sea. David and I fought. I didn't have a full-time home. I pinballed between my parents' house in Georgia and David's apartment in Florida—while he started flight school and I waited to report to The Basic School (TBS). I doubted everything about us. I felt guilty. I felt like I had tainted our relationship. I had been young, holding fast to idyllic beliefs about what an engagement and marriage should be and what life in the Marines meant. We questioned our decision to get married.

Like good Marines, David and I pressed forward. We completed premarital counseling. We worked through our "issues" and decided "if anyone can make it, we can."

Four months later, I returned to Virginia, that time, to Quantico Marine Corps Base. I completed Introductory Flight Screening, during which time David and I got married, and then awaited my start TBS. One day in December, during orientation week of TBS, I sat in one of our classrooms and listened to the JAG describe other incidents of rape and sexual assault that had occurred between Marines at the training school. She was flippant, sarcastic, and insincerely warned us about being careful not to get raped by each other.

I hadn't reported the assault right after it happened because I was so confused. On top of that, I was simply trying to do well on my finals, graduate, get commissioned in the course of the following week, and plan a wedding in a matter of months. I also found myself in a gray area that only Marines can find themselves in—although commissioned, until I reported into TBS, I had no real legal or administrative outlets to contact. However, listening to the JAG brief us about how we were likely going to rape one another at some point in our six-month training program, it hit me, "What if the guy who raped me comes here and does that to someone else? I will never be able to live with myself."

As the JAG told one particular story that sounded eerily similar to mine, I turned my head to the right, and in a room of more than two hundred lieutenants, Laura and I locked eyes. From across the room she mouthed, "You have to tell."

With a heavy heart, I mouthed back, "I know."

The military was notorious for mishandling rape cases, but I felt like it was my duty to report it to possibly protect any potential future victims.

That afternoon, during a break in orientation classes, Laura and I walked to the JAG's office and said we had something to tell her. Even though I explained the timing of reporting the rape, textbook reactions to being raped (bewilderment, shame, guilt, doubt, self-blame), and the content of her brief earlier that day, she seemed surprised and incredulous that I was doing so. I was terrified the legal proceedings would take exactly the route that they did—isolation, fear, repeated questioning that left me feeling like the perpetrator, a disruption of my training cycle, and irrevocable damage to many of my personal relationships, namely my marriage. I reported the rape to the JAG.

At exactly the same time the investigation ensued, I began one of the most rigorous training cycles of my military career, during which time memories of the rape haunted me at every turn. Nearly every day, for months in a row, I had to recall the events of that horrific evening to the JAG, my then-husband, and others involved in the investigation.

I started counseling, hoping that it would equip me to better cope with and understand what I was going through. My father, a retired Air Force Colonel, warned me that seeking mental health support within the military system would damage my career.

"Dad, it's a modern Marine Corps. My commanders have told me it's fine. I'm not suicidal, I'm not homicidal, I'm not on any drugs, and I'm responding to something that happened *to* me. I'm getting great grades and am getting 100 percent on all the physical tests. It'll be okay."

My infantile marriage crumbled like cookies, only not nearly as sweet. We were young, but by anyone's standards, we were a good match and we had taken marriage more seriously than most Marines. We believed we had overcome the obstacle of the rape earlier in the year and had crafted a recipe for success given how much we had in common, how much we loved each other, and how genuinely we believed that we honored the institution of marriage.

We functioned as happy newlyweds, romantically in love with one another, disappointed to be stationed apart, yet confident in the strength of our relationship. We enjoyed a whopping two months as husband and wife before I finally had an opportunity to report the rape. When I presented the facts of the crime to the JAG and moved forward with the legal proceedings, a veritable torture chamber was built around me where each day of questioning was like getting punched directly on a deep, purple-blue bruise.

Even though my husband knew every detail of the story, he demanded that I retell it almost every evening that we talked. It felt like he didn't believe me. It felt like he insisted I repaint the picture in lurid detail time and time again in the hopes that he'd hear some new detail that would make him *really* believe me that I was raped and I hadn't just made a drunken mistake.

Furthermore, the Marine Corps' institutional failure to handle the situation appropriately ripped my scabs open and poured salt directly into the wounds; it was too much to bear. Nothing happened to my assailant. After being half-heartedly promised by the JAG to be kept in the loop, I finally tracked her down one day and had to just ask her in the hallway what happened to my attacker.

She stopped, pivoted toward me, and looked at down me when she said, "Nothing. It's been marked in his records, but no disciplinary or legal action has been taken against him."

My expression begged for an explanation.

"Well, what did you expect under the circumstances?" she said, then turned again and continued her path down the hallway. I stood anchored to that freshly waxed floor and watched her walk away from me with the sharp *click, click, click* of her heels trailing an echo behind her.

That was the only explanation or conclusion I got. I never heard from my MOI or any of my friends still at school ever again.

By all accounts, I was a young, bright, stud of a female officer primed to have a promising career. I'd attended one of the top universities in our country, finishing at the top of my class. I was an athlete. I was a warrior. I was a scholar. I was a top performer throughout college, at Officer Candidate School, and in pretty much everything in which I participated. This worked for me. It comforted my ego. It justified my thoughts, actions, and judgments of myself and others. A product of my upbringing, I utilized external, accomplishment-oriented signals to keep me going. I thought I'd chosen mostly healthy ways to cope. Yet, here I was, barely through the infancy of my career, and things were taking a very different (dark) path from what I envisioned for myself.

Parts of me began to shut down. I wasn't *me* anymore. I was depressed. I was exhausted. I was in physical pain. I didn't want to be touched.

The nightmares I'd had immediately after the rape, which briefly hid in remission for a month or so before and after I married, returned—aggressively—and persisted.

I found myself in the fetal position in the middle of the night—and often during the day—too many times to count. Occasionally I remembered the crawling path I took to get there; other times, there was no distinction between unconsciousness and the real-life nightmare I lived while awake.

I had to lie on my right side because my left side harbored all of my physical injuries and was too painful to even rest upon. The skin of my cheek—hot to the touch yet soaked in sweat (my body's feeble attempt to quell me)—pressed against the chilled tile floor of my bathroom barely big enough to contain my physical form. A baby blue square bore the weight of my cheekbone; an off-white square supported my chin; the soles of my feet grazed the shower curtain. My body formed a "C" as the tops of my thighs pressed against my shattered heart and my arms wrapped forward of my shins, pulling myself into as small of a space as I could imagine. My forehead pressed against my knees. (Sometimes I would repeatedly slam my brow bone against my kneecaps to remind myself a soul still existed inside of that body.) I buried my nose between my legs; it didn't matter that I could barely breathe through the mucus. I tried to wring myself out like a rag, but as my body ached to extract the emotional pain, the only things flowing from my frame were tears. The pain . . . remained.

I went from laughing every day to crying every day. I was not Sarah, and my husband had had enough. I asked him to stick with me through those tough months because I knew it wouldn't last forever. I explained to him that I was having a delayed, but textbook, response to rape. That the poor handling of the case by TBS JAG was exacerbating this grief cycle, but darnit, I was trying my best to suck it up and move on.

"Just give me time," I pleaded.

A few months later, he shrugged his shoulders, raised his hands, palms toward me, and muttered the fateful words that begun the final unraveling, "I can't do it anymore."

We were divorced less than a year later.

Despite the physical and mental anguish I suffered during the six-month crucible, I finished at the top of my class. I graduated from TBS and drove south to Pensacola, Florida: the home of Marine aviation. The initial in-depth flight physical is known as the "NAMI-whammy" because wanna-be pilots are frequently medicinally disqualified for issues that don't come up until they are forced to answer honestly (ideally) a battery of medical questions.

When asked, I answered truthfully that I had employed the psychological counseling options available to me after being raped. I needed help navigating the waters of a stormy marriage as well as the physiological responses to having been raped. My commanders had assured me at the time of said counseling that I would not be penalized for seeking help after being raped because I was not suicidal or homicidal. So, I utilized the resources available to me. I talked to a psychologist about the rape, my divorce, and the fallout. I never took medication or threatened to hurt myself or others. I still got great grades at TBS and performed well—heck, I outperformed most of my male counterparts on many of the physical requirements!

Because I had sought mental health counseling, though, I *was* medically disqualified from flight school. I had grown up hero worshipping my Air Force father who was a C-130 navigator. I traveled extensively as a child and young adult and always loved the plane rides the best. In college I was a member of the Civil Air Patrol, and at TBS I effectively earned my private pilot's license via the Marine Corps' Introductory Flight Screening (IFS) program. Ironically, my cross-country solo flight during IFS was to Charlottesville and back, and when I landed there it was the first time I'd returned since graduating. I was good at flying. I enjoyed it. I planned to commit at least eight years to the Corps if not twenty.

But I was disqualified from even trying to accomplish my goal. The dream I had of becoming a pilot died along with my marriage and parts of my soul.

I drank heavily, but disguised it amidst the party culture of Pensacola pilots and post-college coeds who populated the beach town. After a whole lot of prayer and mentorship, I moved forward from (not starting) flight school and went to Intelligence Officer School in Dam Neck, Virginia (where I was hit by a car while riding my bike and suffered my tenth traumatic brain injury at that point in my life). Three weeks after graduating that school, I deployed to Iraq for seven months. I was home for a few months, then deployed to Iraq for a second time.

I was deeply disappointed with, and utterly wounded by the institution, which not only let me down, but continued to punish me in one way or another for years afterward for having reported the rape. Every time the counseling paperwork resurfaced when I changed units, I had to tell the story again, so my commanders always knew about it but would tell me it didn't color their opinion of me because I was a top performer. But words and reality are sometimes different, and my career *was* colored by the "rape" paintbrush in one shade or another for nearly seven years. "It" followed me like a black cloud throughout my Marine Corps career. Sometimes the cloud rained; other times, it was just there hovering, omnipresent.

At one command in particular, reporting unrelated harassment (which to be honest, is just a disturbingly common issue for female Marines), resulted in the rape being resurrected as a conversation piece. The idea was to discredit me as a *complainer*, that most loathsome of labels in the Corps. The rape was the rationale used for doubt of *anything* I said because even though it was a prevalent reality in military ranks, "it" was still referred to as if military rape were a myth to be dispelled. It felt worse later, though, while I was in a combat zone. I was away from family. I had been separated from the whole. I was a pariah, separated from my unit. I drifted.

Although I never planned to take my own life, I wanted it taken from me. I was done. I stopped eating, not because I forcefully denied myself nourishment as a form of control or punishment, but because I had lost my appetite; I had lost my will to live. Like an animal does when it knows it's time to go, I allowed time to take its own course with me. I faded. I was an athletic 5'6" young woman fading below 120 pounds who never slept, was kept awake by the nightmares of the rape years before as well as the current harassment, and felt I had no purpose on this earth. I returned to that familiar "C" shape in my tiny room that was only large enough for a single bed, a closet, and a yoga mat.

I began sporadically practicing yoga in college to deal with overtraining injuries from soccer and ROTC, but it was nothing more than creative cross-training to me. With even consciously processing the transformation, when I was emotionally distraught, yoga gave me clarity. The simple, basic union of breath and movement made space for something very important—my soul. Somehow, when I felt like I was suffocating, my soul had space to breathe. Somehow, in a body experiencing very physical effects of depression, when I practiced yoga, I had less pain. Somehow, in a world that felt like 24/7 chaos, the mat gave me an anchor point. All of my systems integrated in a way that allowed me to keep functioning when simply surviving seemed impossible. Somewhere buried within, I knew I was still there for a reason, even if I didn't fully understand it yet.

I spent at least the next two years, still on active duty in the Marines, pickling my judgment with booze, fast and furious relationships, thrill seeking, and temper tantrums. Yet, I appeared (mostly) healthy to friends as far as I knew.

It wasn't *all* bad . . . I also reconnected to faith-based groups while I lived in California and Virginia, I continued to run triathlons, I got back to playing soccer again (and ended up playing for the US Military Olympic team for five years in a row), and I learned how to surf.

I also had my faith. Ah, my faith; its form had evolved, but it was still my anchor. I had succumbed to depression in a very physical, literal way for a while there, in addition to the musculoskeletal problems I already had from injuries and various stressors. My body articulated the complaints and unrest that my voice could not in form of everything from migraines to amenorrhea. I'd had some healthy relationships and a few poisonous ones. I had the sensation of never really being able to catch my breath from 2003 to 2009. I felt like given everything I'd been through, I should've been dead. But I wasn't. And there had to be a reason. My faith is what helped me believe there was a reason, even if I didn't know the scope of it yet.

It took several years to realize the power of choice I had in how I could respond, act, and live with my rape. In many ways, my "dealing with" the rape was less about the rape and more about the fallout. My life wasn't ruined, but some serious dreams had been dashed and relationships lost, and I struggled with nightmares, depression, erratic mood swings, and loss of hope sporadically for several years along with consistently poor health throughout. I thought about what it would be like to die, enough that it terrified me. The institutional letdown felt deeply personal. I couldn't become a pilot, so I became an Intelligence

Officer but even that career took a hit during the aftermath of my second deployment, and I was unable to fully pursue the lengthy Marine Corps career I had dreamed of in the way I had envisioned. I could have stayed in, but it didn't feel authentic anymore. I was called a liar, a whore, a bitch, a dyke, a victim, crazy, weirdo, psycho, and more. But those are just names, not who I am.

I was raped. Yes. I was divorced. Yup. I was lost. But I was still *Sarah* in there somewhere. Over time, I evolved.

Because of these trials, I now live, love, and serve more fully than I ever thought possible back in 2003 on the cusp of Marinehood. When I left the Marines, service in a whole new way began for me, and so did the rest of my life.

I traveled the world for nearly a year, doing volunteer work in the Middle East and Europe, and traveling solo and with friends across six continents and forty countries. I returned to the Washington DC area and found a great job with an intelligence contractor. I worked there for a year before giving into the urging of friends and family to write a book, speak, and coach based on my personal and professional experiences.

I've stepped into the "light" of advocacy, of speaking to, instructing, and inspiring others to see obstacles as opportunities because I've walked through the fires and lived to tell. I don't take personal credit for being where I am now because I know it's oh so much bigger than little ol' me. This realization also helps me accept that the "bad stuff" is beyond me too, and that allows me to be at peace about it all. Everything that I've gone through has molded me into the person I am now and propelled me forward to build the businesses I have.

I am honored to speak on behalf of other survivors of sexual violence. I feel humbled when I hear from strangers that my voice has given them hope. When I hear from a young woman my age, a prior Marine, who I spent thirty minutes chatting with one night at a seminar: "You have no idea how impactful our brief meeting was on my life. You are truly an inspiration to me" or a woman at a Wounded Warrior Project retreat that "because you went through some of the same things I have, and you made it through it, I know I can too," then I know it's all been worth it. To receive thanks from senators' Chiefs of Staff is just plain awesome.

I am excited to learn more and more about integrative nutrition and holistic health care practices because sharing that healing with others is a priceless gift. I am brought to tears when men and women I hold in high esteem tell me that my writing has inspired them and they want to share it with their children, friends, and colleagues. I struggle to find the words to express my gratitude for yoga as a healing art for saving my life on more than one occasion, and the saviors—Christian, yogic, and secular—who have accompanied those savings. Yoga allows me to express my service and faith to an extent I cherish in a modality I enjoy. So, to list my business accomplishments of the last year is not a ticker of ego biscuits but a scroll of gratitude for God, love, compassion, friends, and continually improving health.

And it's not all sunshine and butterflies these days. Although I've left the military, I now move in nonprofit and civilian circles where I find that the past never stays completely in the past, both by my own choice to share my story as well as violently forced upon me, as I was reminded a couple years ago. A veteran nonprofit contacted me to tell me they had decided to bestow a prestigious award upon me. It was all good to go; I just needed to have a conversation with the executive director of the organization to confirm it. During that call, I was aggressively and repeatedly told and asked in various ways, "You are branding yourself as a rape victim. Why are you doing that? I know most women just make up rape stories. The statistics are lies. I was a leader of a unit and there were no reports of rape while I was in command." He spoke in accusations and questions for at least ten minutes uninterrupted.

As I sat silent on my end of the phone, receiving his bullets of doubt, I was emotionally triggered. It felt disgustingly familiar. I was transported back in time and was mildly sick for a week or so after his calls. My back and hips ached. My nightmares returned.

I declined the award. Thankfully, after an angry follow-up e-mail from him I was able to close my laptop and take myself to my meditation pillow. I was grounded. I had a resource. As a peaceful warrior I knew that retaliating in anger would serve no purpose. But don't get me wrong; I felt plenty of anger!

From the questions, the fears, the conflicts, the shaky foundations, the drama, and the pain, I've been propelled forward in beautiful ways to craft my life in a way I design. I make a very special effort to keep in touch with people who I love and who love me. I'm married to an incredible man and for the first time can picture a life of stability without getting scared. I want it. I need it. I deserve it. I accept that patterns in our lives repeat until we learn. I accept that my parents did the best they could at the level of consciousness they had, from the experiences they had. I retroactively conceptually understand that about the Marine Corps as well—like an abusive father or boyfriend, I kept with "him" because I did love "him," rightfully so because he treated me well at times. Growing up rootless is certainly part of what lured me into the arms of the Marine Corps, for we seek what we know and somehow the Marines offered me both roots in uniformity and heritage while simultaneously keeping me nomadic.

But the time came to say good-bye . . . then to let go . . . then to move forward . . . and now to live, live, live, LOVE, and burn brightly with joy. Thank you for sharing time and space with me on these pages.

### *End of Warning*

In order to forgive and forget something or someone, in order to not hate it or hate them and let that hate live in your heart and destroy you, you have to let go. We simply cannot allow ourselves to hate. We must choose love or else we end up dying while we're living. I chose to embrace the joy, love, and happiness in my life. No one wants to be in a relationship—personally or professionally—with someone who is angry or bitter. Heck, you don't want to be in a relationship with *yourself* when you're in that state of mind and state of heart. I don't say this to make light of my own or others' traumas. It really boiled down to realizing I had a choice for *how* to live my life. Some say courage isn't the absence of fear but action despite that fear. Living a full, happy life after trauma is sort of like that. Choosing to live out of love instead of out of fear or anger is not due to an absence of trauma but in spite of it.

Some very dark things have happened to many of us. Yet, we all have the potential within us to find the bright side of survival and be grateful that we are still alive and truly able to make of our lives what we wish.

Here are some suggestions I hope you find helpful. I call them my Requirements for Resiliency:

1. *Replace self-defeating thoughts with positive ones,* with ones that create positive energy to move forward, as well as ones that allow you to find points of flexibility and build balance.

*"Most people are about as happy as they make up their minds to be."*
—Abraham Lincoln

2. *Own your life.* Identify all beliefs, decisions, and actions as your own. Do not be content to merely survive; know that you were born to strive. You are in charge of you. You have the power of choice in everything, especially in relation to resiliency.

*You are all children of the light and children of the day. We do not belong to the night or to the darkness.*
—1 Thessalonians 5:5

3. *Follow through by reinforcing success, not failure.* At The Basic School, we learned this lesson of intention—although it was not referred to as such—in regards to a combat setting, but it holds true for life. Where your thoughts go, your intention flows. If you focus on the things that are going wrong or the mistakes you have made, you are reinforcing failure. Find what works for you and put your energy there!

*"Identify your problems, but give your power and energy to solutions."*
—Tony Robbins

4. *Get outside your comfort zone.* Exemplify a willingness to push your own limits to get beyond a struggle. Be a problem solver, not a problem wallower. Leading by example is often uncomfortable—but worthwhile—work.

*"No matter what he does, every person on earth plays a central role in the history of the world. And normally he doesn't know it."*
—Paulo Coelho, *The Alchemist*

5. *Let go of your attachment to past pain because attachment is the root of your struggles.* If you can, even in very small ways, release pieces of the pain, you can grow a spirit of resilience. Being sincere in your endeavors, empathetic toward others, motivated to make the world a better place, and excited about your future, with humor, you can become resilient.

   *"Don't sweat the petty things, and don't pet the sweaty things."*

   —George Carlin

6. *Get over the idea of controlling everything or having certainty.* Uncertainty is actually often a gift that directs us toward having to trust our intuition and rely on our God.

   *"Certainty comes by using your gifts, by allowing your power to change your world. Forgiveness of your own past is the starter and then work with all your love."*

   —Agni

7. *Be courageous, compassionate, and vulnerable!* Have the courage to be imperfect and the compassion to forgive yourself first, then others. Vulnerability is also required because although vulnerability is neither easy nor excruciating, it is necessary, and as you allow for openness, you allow for greater connection. Connection fuels resiliency, because when you become disconnected you lose hope. Courage, vulnerability, and connection keep us afloat.

   *"What we give our attention to—stays with us. What we let go of—will let go of us."*

   —Cat Forsley

8. *Force less; flow more. Accept that ultimately, everything is temporary.* Compulsive thought, worry, or dread will only make it worse. Why NOT let it go? As soon as you start accepting change, you start to end the suffering.

*"It takes a lot of courage to release the familiar and seemingly secure, to embrace the new. But there is no real security in what is no longer meaningful. There is more security in the adventurous and exciting, for in movement there is life, and in change there is power."*

—Alan Cohen

9. *Believe that your trials did not arrive to punish you, but to teach you.* What might seem like unbearable loads, insurmountable problems, and constant drama are actually invitations for introspection and change. It is a matter of perspective—you don't have to be thrilled about crappy things happening. You can see them as an opportunity. Resilient people are not those who have not suffered, but those who have. They've faced it and made a choice to move beyond it—to make lemon pie from lemons. Happiness is a result of accepting what is. What you resist, persists. Acceptance is not complacency; it simply means choosing your thoughts.

*"Only to the extent that we expose ourselves over and over to annihilation can that which is indestructible in us be found."*

—Pema Chodron

10. *You must be healthy in order to heal.* Incorporate health and wellness into your resiliency plan; one cannot exist without the other. Emotional and mental resiliency is a lost cause without physical resiliency. Health can be a gateway to spiritual well-being. To paraphrase a comment I heard Dr. Van der Kolk make one time, "To change how you feel, move your body."

*"Health is a state of complete harmony of the body, mind and spirit. When one is free from physical disabilities and mental distractions, the gates of the soul open."*

—BKS Iyengar

11. *Fortify yourself: don't just weight train—spirit train!* Just as you would weight train to build strength, you can spirit train to build resiliency. You can deal with the unexpected effectively through preparation (not control). This principle is closely

tied to that of #10. For instance, consider reading books that diverge from your typical thought process, have conversations with people who challenge you, or try incorporating meditation or daily movement or exercise. Take the time to nourish your relationships, career, spirituality, happiness, intuition, and physical fitness into your life in such a way that they are not chores or to-do's, but critical elements and second nature to your self-care regimen.

*"Spiritual life is like a medicinal herb: bitter in the beginning, sweet in the end. Becoming conscious can initially be challenging. But once you get rolling, your life becomes peaceful, blissful, and much sweeter for your efforts."*
—Steve Ross, *Happy Yoga*

Yoga saved my life on my second deployment, and its life-saving qualities are exactly what continue to make me passionate about sharing it with others. The days I felt as if I were suffocating, I could go to my mat and simply breathe . . . and since breath is life, it kept me living. Although at first I thought yoga was just a bunch of "hippie hocus pocus," had I not finally opened up to the idea of trying it, I may have never discovered its life-enhancing qualities. Yoga provides a physical method for expressing our spiritual growth. *It takes big, meaningful, and usually ethereal concepts, and puts them in our bodies so we can experience them.* The postures are not about what we can literally do; the movement is about the movement, the growth happening within. As I heard Dr. Bessel van Der Kolk say recently at the Omega Institute, *"Nothing will change until you move."*

Perception and choice are crucial components to a healthy mind-set. Can we choose to perceive a situation differently than we are conditioned? Are we more than just sleepwalkers? Victims? Mindless eaters? Reactionaries? We cannot undo what's already been done, or insert into the past the things that have not been done. We can only start where we are, here, today, present, ready for more of life, and be willing to just roll with it and move forward. We must take ownership over our lives and not be content to merely survive; we need to know with every fiber in our beings that we are born to thrive.

*"In the middle of difficulty lies opportunity."*

—Albert Einstein

Experiences are cyclical, rolling like a wheel through life. What we put out into the world will come back around to us, will be mirrored to us, and put before us in the areas in which we still need growth. Let's learn from the journey, not begrudge it! Aspire to stay flexible and fluid through acceptance of the dark or difficult times, and you will be on your way to a resilient, happy life!

## Roll Call: Resilient

*"In three words I can sum up everything I've learned about life. It goes on."*

—Robert Frost

1. Who are your resilient "roll" models? What about them do you admire? Why do you consider them resilient? Have they inspired you to be resilient?
2. Is there a mentor, role model, leader, or coach in your past who has guided you through a tough time? How big of a part did they play in your living out your resilience?
3. What would you need to do to improve and deepen the sense of resilience you have in relation to yourself and others?
4. What is something that happened in your life that, at the time, you felt as though it would last forever and which has now passed? How do you feel about it now?
5. What is a situation in which you have found the "silver lining?" Is there an opportunity that has arisen that you originally saw as an obstacle? Resiliency means returning to "original form." How have you stayed true to your real you?
6. Roll with resilience by accepting and embracing that change is constant by reminding yourself that nothing lasts forever, by believing that you have the power to change your life and taking action to do so, and by pursuing health as a priority—not as an afterthought—because good health is vital to your ability to obtain a *lasting* healing.

## OFFERING: Prayer or meditation

Allow yourself to come to a place of stillness and comfort, sitting on the floor or on a chair with both feet flat on the floor.

» If possible, be somewhere quiet and without distractions and give yourself a moment to just settle in.

» If sounds, distractions, or sensations arise, do your best to integrate them into the practice.

» Then begin to inhale and exhale just through your nose, allowing the inhale to be a little longer than the exhale.

» If you'd like to count, try counting six on the inhale and four on the exhale.

» You may feel yourself building a little energy.

» Then do your best to recall a time that you bounced back from something, that you rose stronger than you were before.

» As you're able to do so, keep the memory simple and hone in on one or two aspects of your own inherent strengths and gifts that empowered you to resiliently recover after that tough time.

» Then meditate on those traits for a few minutes, keeping your breath smooth, deep, and even.

» You may even want to repeat, "I am resilient."

# Chapter 10

# CONCLUSION: JUST ROLL WITH IT

*"I want to keep my soul fertile for the changes, so things keep getting born in me, so things keep dying when it is time for things to die. I want to keep walking away from the person I was a moment ago, because a mind was made to figure things out, not to read the same page recurrently."*
—Donald Miller, *Through Painted Deserts*

After I left active duty in July of 2009, I set out to travel the world. What was originally supposed to be just a couple of months abroad turned into nearly a year of traveling alone, as well as with friends, some of whom were old friends and some made along the way. There were a few times I came home between trips during that year, though, one of which was in the fall of 2009 for a close friend's wedding, which I simply couldn't miss, even if it meant flying home from Europe to attend.

I had been living in the DC area since 2007. Between Arlington, Fairfax County, and DC proper, I was a member of a handful of adult intramural soccer teams. One team had a game the weekend I was home. I hadn't played in a few months. I figured, why not, I'll go out, have a run around, see some friends, and have some fun.

Since I'd been out of the country, a few new girls had joined the team. I was playing forward with one of said new girls. She was about my size, a little more petite, blond, and quick. She was fun to play with, and we were connecting on the field, passing to one another and generating scoring opportunities.

I was having a blast. It was a beautiful fall day, I was home from Europe enjoying soccer with friends, I was feeling happier and happier each day I was out of the Marine Corps, and although I'd just broken up with a serious boyfriend, all in all, things were good. The creases by my eyes deepened, both from the sun and my smile, as I jogged up and down the turf field. I was in my element and grateful to be there.

The other team kicked the ball out of bounds and it rolled down the little hill bordering our pitch, making a beeline for the parking lot. A short, athletic man darted toward the ball and grabbed it before it ended up in the nearby road. He threw it up the hill to one of my teammates gesturing with open arms.

I lurched to a stop. I stared. My jaw dropped. That man was my *ex-husband*. I hadn't seen him since 2006, when he jumped on a helicopter to catch a ride to Al Taqaddam to see me the second time we were both deployed to Iraq.

I was playing soccer in the sunshine like a little kid yet simultaneously drumming up images of a combat zone. Although I was in Virginia, memories of Iraq were here and now, and the recollection of that last personal interaction with him flashed through my mind. We had spent nearly the whole day together that day in 2006. That evening, we sat on the roof of the building where I lived. The sunsets in Iraq were beautiful. As ugly as everything else often was around us, those sunsets were always beautiful gifts from God. We had sat in silence for a while, but once the conversation began, it was an outpouring.

Prior to that night, the last time my ex-husband and I had seen each other was also in Iraq, but in 2005. That time I'd been the one to catch a flight on a helicopter to see him in Fallujah. Then, too, after some silence, our conversation was an outpouring of tears and memories. He had been adamant about us getting back together. We'd been divorced for a year or two at that point, yet he still believed we could be the "All-American couple." But we were in a combat zone then too, and as erratic as my behavior often was, even I knew that was a silly place to make such serious declarations. We promised each other we'd stay in touch, and if we were ever in the same state again, we would try to spend some time together. Or if things went on and we ever got to the point of being engaged to someone else, we'd let the other person know.

Back to that night in 2006 . . . as we watched the sun set, we had about an hour or so before I had to drive him to the JACOT (a.k.a. the military airport). We agreed that we were really going to move on with our lives, yet somehow we felt as though we might still end up back together. We agreed that maybe when we were back in the States, if we weren't dating anyone, we would have lunch. We'd start there.

We tried to be strong, but when it came time for him to leave, we both cried, hugged, sat apart, cried again, hugged again, and finally he got out of the car and walked away. His small, strong frame in his desert cammies, attempting to make him look like every other Marine in-country, yet his specific gait—one that more closely resembled his big, generous heart and his warm confidence—forever distinguishing him in my subconscious mind.

That was the last time I saw him.

Several months after that meeting in Iraq in late 2006, we had returned from our respective deployments and were both living in California in early 2007. We tried to get together a couple times, but the conversations to coordinate were uncharacteristically tense, short, and somewhat combative. I was confused and hurt. When we'd met up in Iraq in 2005, he was so adamant about us getting back together.

When we met up in Iraq again in 2006, I was dating someone else, but everything was amicable between us. We had spoken *again* of possibly getting back together. We had maintained the type of relationship that surprised many. I had one of my close friends, and fellow Marine, say that she'd never seen two ex-spouses speak so highly of one another. Our good-bye in 2006 was long and drawn out with hugs and tears and talking of the past and future.

Therefore, in 2007, when we were both finally back in the US—in the very same state, no less—and he blew me off over trying to get together for lunch, I was wounded. I reacted poorly to his rejection. I was suffering from PTSD, depression, and erratic mood swings. I probably said "Screw you then, don't call me again," or something really mature and compassionate. I had no tools in my toolbox to deal with my emotions in any other way than anger and defensiveness.

I'd called and written a few times since my outburst, apologizing and wishing him well. I never got a response. I gradually released any hope of seeing him again, let alone discussion of reunification. Then in early 2008, I heard a rumor that he might be assigned to my same unit in Quantico, Virginia. I called him at his work number to let him know I was at said unit in Quantico in case that would affect his decision. No animosity, just information. He was pretty matter-of-fact on the phone, saying he knew, and he appreciated me calling. That was it.

In 2009 when I *just so happened* to be home from Europe, just so happened to be playing in *that* game at *that* field at *that* time, and he *just so happened to be* the random dude who chased a ball down, I was stunned. He has a very distinct body type, figure, and manner of walking, so when I saw him run after the ball that afternoon, before I saw his face, I knew who it was. When he then turned and threw the ball up to my teammate, I stood rooted to the ground for a moment, doing nothing. I tried to make eye contact with him and quasi-wave, but we were in the middle of a game so I couldn't do much.

Play resumed. I watched him walk from the parking lot side of the field, around the back of our goal, toward our sideline. I would make a pass, and then look over toward him again. I would jog up the field, and glance over toward him. I was in intel mode, trying to gather any information I possibly could at all.

*Did he see my car and stop by to say hi?* I wondered. *Is he here visiting a friend? Is he in one of these leagues and is playing soon?*

My silent questions were answered when I saw him talking to the new girl with whom I'd been playing forward. They chatted, and based on their body language, I thought, *Oh no big deal, she's just a friend, or maybe they just started dating.* Not that his relationship status really mattered, but that's what crossed my mind.

The halftime whistle blew. I jogged toward him and practically shouted, "Hey! How are you? What're you doin' here?" A small tremor buzzed through my body.

I opened my arms and leaned toward him.

He extended his hand. In monotone, he said, "Hi Sarah. Nice to see you."

My shock compounded. He was acting like a robot.

"What're you doin' here?" I asked again.

"Oh, um . . . ya, I'm just here . . . with, um . . . my *fiancé.*"

I'm surprised I didn't throw up then and there.

"Oh, okay, cool," I said. I tried to appear normal and continue the conversation. I asked him where he was stationed now, how his mom and grandmother were, stuff like that. He provided one-word answers. I told him I was out of the Marines now and home from traveling. He appeared disinterested. I had Bailey there, tied up to the bleachers, and I wanted to introduce him to Bailey because Teddy had been such a big part of our lives together. For some reason, I kept thinking I needed to introduce him to Bailey. But I never got the chance. The robot conversation ended. We said our good-byes.

I walked over to my team captain and told her I had to make a phone call real quick. I jogged to my car. *No big deal. It's whatever; I'm just going to make a phone call.*

I picked up my cell phone and held the number 2 down. My mom picked up. And I started bawling. The tears weren't about the fact that he was engaged again; they were over the memories flooding me, suffocating me at that moment. I felt consumed by memories as if they were happening in the present moment. I associated the divorce with the rape. The two wounds were inextricably tied in my heart's memory. The pain-filled years, the stressful deployments, the harassment and crap I went through in the Marines, flashes of tearful conversations and gut-wrenching fights, were all there in the car with me.

*"Holding on to anything is like holding on to your breath. You will suffocate. The only way to get anything in the physical universe is by letting go of it. Let go and it will be yours forever."*

—Deepak Chopra

As happy as I was in October 2009—exactly six years after I'd been married, although we were divorced a year later—I was a long way away from healed, and I certainly didn't know how to "just roll with it" in all circumstances yet. I was still slightly "stuck" with some internal emotional and physical battles, but out of the Marines, traveling, healing bit by bit, and in the process of getting "unstuck." Even so, when I was "unstuck" in those early years out, it was easy for things like that to put me right back in my stuck place.

I spent the day on the phone with my mom, my sister, and my best friends, relaying the play-by-play of how things went down. I cried quite a bit with my mom and sister, less with my best girlfriends, and even began chuckling as I told the story to my buddies. Before the day was over, I was laughing about it. How small did the world have to be that of all the soccer leagues in the DC area, of all the teams, of all the positions, my ex-husband's new fiancé and I were playing forward together on a soccer team, and he happened to show up to her game the one weekend I was home from world travel? I understand now that God puts things like this in our path to teach us the lessons that still need learning.

*"You will only be sent more and more teachers, each more intense than the previous one. Your task is to learn the lesson that the teacher has for you rather than to resent the teacher."*
—Carolyn Myss, *Anatomy of the Spirit*

Don't worry, I did learn . . . eventually. When I returned from traveling, I did not switch teams (as many of my friends told me I should do). My ex-husband showed up at another game or two, and his new fiancé and I continued to play together, often high-fiving one another as we assisted each other's goals and served one another good passes. It never bothered me *on* the field—I was definitely just rolling with it—but sometimes it would hit me after the game. I was still a little sad about it all. On some level, I still mourned the loss of what he and I had when we were so young, before the tragedies started falling like dominoes in our young married life: rape, fighting, marriage, legal battle, living separately, impending deployments, fighting, making up, fighting, making up, divorcing, seeing each other in a combat zone, and on and on and on. So, I'd let myself sit with those emotions for a bit, maybe cry or talk to a friend, then that was it. There was nothing else to do or anything else to hold onto. I would remind myself to accept what had happened, have faith that the journey served a purpose, and do what I could to learn from the situation and move forward in a positive way. If I stayed in those painful memories of the past, I got sick in every sense of the word, and frankly, I couldn't afford to keep living that way—which was dying.

*"Everybody has to change, or they expire."*
—Donald Miller, *Through Painted Deserts*

That is why I wrote this book for you: because it is actually a matter of life and death. You know what's really scary? I'll tell you what: living a life of complacency, of depression, of mediocrity. *Fear and pain is what causes that totally ridiculous acceptance of the blasé for most of us.*

It's your life, darnit! Face what it is you're scared of and take it head on. Don't you want to live it to your fullest potential?

Many of us are dying inside. God knows I was for years! But I promise it does not have to be that way. And as I hope to be a living, breathing, jumping, laughing, traveling, ridiculous fool of an imperfect example to you so that you can make your life what you want it to be, you too should be that inspiration to others.

Each of you reading this book is reading it for a reason. There is something you are supposed to learn from it, whether it be from my experience or from examining your own life. Begin to believe—or *strengthen* your belief—that you have the power to choose your approach to life. Subsequently, your attitude will drive your action. *Now* is the time to get unstuck in whatever way that applies to your beautiful life. The world *needs* your message. I challenge you to go out there into the world and accept, serve, and inspire others.

The life I have built for myself now is beautiful one for which I don't take for granted for a second. I am not sure I would appreciate it as much as I do, though, if not for the hard times I have been through. It is easier for me to move forward recognizing that the future is an unknown, yet taking heart in the resiliency I've cultivated, which is based on faith, authenticity, and perseverance. I find excitement—not fear—in the unknown now. Although, to be forthright, this attitude is still a work in progress for me too; resiliency is a muscle that requires maintenance and exercise.

So, get to flexin' your resiliency muscle, and get to writing the next chapter of your own life story. You got this!

> *"Embrace relational uncertainty. It's called romance. Embrace spiritual uncertainty. It's called mystery. Embrace occupational uncertainty. It's called destiny. Embrace emotional uncertainty. It's called joy. Embrace intellectual uncertainty. It's called revelation."*
>
> —Mark Batterson

By no means is this an exhaustive list. I hope that some of the examples encourage you along the way, though. All elements of SEMPER are interrelated, integrated, exist on a spectrum, and require practice.

Remember, this is how we "Just Roll With It."

1.  Have faith.

*"As you begin to see the twists and turns—those surprising events and circumstances that happen for a reason you are not yet aware of—you'll realize that everything that happens to you is part of a perfect plan designed especially for your personalized, Life 101 course."*

—Kristine Carlson

> How do you know you've applied it? You don't worry as much, you have a sense of peace and contentment even amidst chaos and stress, and you find yourself attracting more positive people and events.

2.  Be sincere in all you think, feel, and do. Listen to all the ways that you know that you know, and ask more questions when you know that you don't know.

*"Your time is limited, so don't waste it living someone else's life. Don't be trapped by dogma—which is living with the results of other people's thinking. Don't let the noise of other's opinions drown out your own inner voice. And most importantly, have the courage to follow your heart and intuition. They somehow already know what you truly want to become. Everything else is secondary."*

—Steve Jobs

> How do you know you've applied it? You don't have to *think* so hard about what to say or do; you feel confident in simply *being* who you are. Your relationships with others improve as your sense of self matures and your fulfillment deepens. Your intuition is firing on all cylinders in all areas of your life: spirituality, relationships, career, fitness, and health.

3.  Empathize with others to make their place and yours in this world that much better.

*"Take the focus off yourself and imagine what it's like to be in someone else's predicament, and simultaneously feel love for that person. It's the recognition that other people's problems, their pain and frustrations, are every bit as real as our own—often far worse."*

—Dr. Richard Carlson

How do you know you've applied it? You find yourself more aware of others' feelings and circumstances and treat them with less judgment and more forgiveness and kindness. Those with whom you are closest will likely notice a positive change, and your relationships will become even closer. You don't find yourself feeling as angry or frustrated by things that would normally frazzle you because you exude gratitude for the blessings you do have. Also, you honor your boundaries and those of others.

4. Embrace your inner drive and be on a quest to live a motivated life!

*"Courage is a door that can only be opened from the inside."*

—Terry Neil

How do you know you've applied it? People begin coming to you more and more for advice, inspiration, and instruction. You feel enlivened by your work—professionally and personally— and like you are on the path you are supposed to be on.

5. Persevere and overcome any obstacle put in your path.

*"We must do the things we think we cannot do."*—*Eleanor Roosevelt.* *Remember that "Problems are opportunities in work clothes."*

—Unknown

Perseverance must be meant with grace, gratitude, and rest and recovery, as well.

How do you know you've applied it? You are not easily swayed when you hit a bump in the road. Because your purpose and motivation are strong, you are able to stay the course. You are mindful of the bigger picture and are strengthened by the power you have to decide who you will be and what your life

177

will be like. Likewise, within that mindfulness, you become more and more adept at knowing when to do less so that you give yourself a chance to recover and rebuild.

6.   Get amped up, stay engaged with others, be present, and connect.

*"When you have once seen the glow of happiness on the face of a beloved person, you know that a man can have no vocation but to awaken that light on the faces surrounding him. In the depth of winter, I finally learned that within me there lay an invincible summer."*

—Albert Camus

Be excited, grateful, and happy about the gift that life is.

"I have chosen to be happy because it is good for my health."—Voltaire

How do you know you've applied it? Connecting with others becomes increasingly effortless; it doesn't feel like a chore, rather you find joy in your personal and professional relationships again. Synchronicity starts happening more often, and positive "coincidences" keep popping up. You don't feel distracted when you talk and interact with people because you are fully present. You feel mentally fresh and energetically excited. You want to get up in the morning.

7.   Take comfort in your innate capacity for resilience. Give time and energy to your strengths, time and space to your pain, and patience and grace in your healing. Resilience includes rest and recovery too! We cannot go 100 mph at all times.

How do you know you've applied it? Crap has happened but you're still living your life. You see obstacles as opportunities wrapped in an ugly brown, lumpy, wet cardboard box—it is still a gift; it just didn't come packaged the way you would've preferred. Your perspective shifts to where you resent challenges less and see them more as chances for growth; you are aware that there is a lesson you need to learn, so you are a student about the matter instead of a "Negative Nancy." You are unshakeable because you stay true to your core character regardless of what's going on around you.

8.  Get moving. After cultivating these seven traits, we must be bold, be brave, take action, and move forward in order to truly live out the "Just Roll With It" motto.

*"Let him who would move the world, first move himself."*

—Socrates

How do you know you've applied it? You take heart in knowing that agency is possible sometimes through even the smallest of choices within your realm of possible. Most of the time, you can actually apply the principle of "let go and let God" not just talk about it and say, "I know I should 'let go and let God, but I don't.'" This is the same idea of nonattachment that yogis discuss and practice. You have a sensation of freedom and gratitude. You choose optimism over pessimism. You are able to move forward physically, mentally, emotionally, and spiritually. Things just seem to *flow* and you feel healthy, happy, and successful.

Movement in all areas of life means not focusing on the past or the future, but being fully present in the fluidity of now.

Also, it means that literally, you should physically move each day. As a society, we are an entirely too stagnant, and it reflects in our personalities and outlooks on life. Research shows that all major experts and gurus do something to get moving at the start of their day. That means athletes, yogis, thought leaders, and spiritual leaders all incorporate some element of movement into their day, so I suggest you do too. Don't get stuck in thought; get moving in action. Accept where you are, ask for help where need be, and expose and open yourself to receive the help that may come.

All the SEMPER traits are not ones to be had or not had; they're practices! They are states of mind and states of the spirit that become action and behavior. Resilience builds through repeated choices, which is how practice works.

You weren't born knowing how to tie your shoes. The first time you tried to tie your shoes, you probably failed miserably at it, then you tried again, and again, and again. Then, one day you could actually tie your shoes. Now, tying your shoes is like second nature; you can do it with your eyes closed. Resilience practice is like that. It's going to be hard at first. Keep trying.

> *"The first step to living the life you want is leaving the life you don't want. Taking the first step forward is always the hardest, but then each step forward gets easier and easier and each step forward gets you closer and closer until eventually what had once been invisible starts to be visible, and what had once felt impossible starts to feel possible."*
>
> —Karen Salmansohn

*Choose* to live the life you love and love the life you live no matter what!

Be a light to others:

> *"To know that even one life has breathed easier because you have lived, that is to have succeeded."*
>
> —Ralph Waldo Emerson

Now, let's roll!

# Roll Call: Conclusion

*"Simply being more aware of imbalance is the first step to becoming more balanced."*

—Paul Pitchford, MS

Now that you have completed the book, Q&As, and practiced applying the lessons learned about the seven core traits of happy, healthy, successful people, fill out the SEMPER Wheel again and see what has changed.

Moving forward, use the SEMPER Wheel as your personal checklist. When making a decision, facing a crossroad, or feeling lost in a challenge, ask yourself: Does this course of action build my faith, or tear it down? Is this sincere, or do I feel this is misaligned with my core sense of self somehow? Am I being empathetic toward myself or others through this action? What is my motivation, why am I doing this, do I feel connected to my purpose? Will this course of action build perseverance, is it sustainable, or will I burn out? Am I truly engaged in and excited about this course of action? Does it build my resilience? Can I really live with my choice or action and Just Roll With It?

# OFFERING: Prayer or Meditation

Find a comfortable position, either sitting, lying down, or perhaps even resting comfortably on your side with support underneath you. Allow yourself to settle into this position.

- » Then, close your eyes if you feel comfortable doing so.
- » Take a couple slow breaths.
- » Call to mind something—a feeling, a relationship, a sensation, a habit, a thought—that you want to let go of.
- » See it in your mind's eye.
- » Try not to get too complicated with yourself and pick just one thing for now. Visualize it as a small candle.
- » Then imagine lighting the candle.
- » See a river in front of you; go to that river.
- » Kneel down and gently place your candle in that river.

» Say a prayer or offering before letting it go, then watch it slowly float away with the current of the water. Continue to watch the candle float away.

Remember, letting go is a process. "Just Roll With It" may sound flippant, but it is not. Release takes time. It is a practice. You can return to this visualization daily and see how the imagery changes or remains the same. Let it be a practice that meets you where you are.

*"Having faith sometimes means trusting that beautiful things can and will arise from something ugly, not just when bad things happen to us but also when we make mistakes. Because when God whispers and you miss it, He shouts, and if you don't hear Him, He shakes, rattles, and rolls you. He wants your attention because He wants to help, and ultimately, ". . . he will command his angels concerning you to guard you in all your ways" (Psalm 91:11).*

—Sarah Plummer Taylor

# JUST ROLL WITH IT MANIFESTO

We Just Roll With It because . . .

- ✓ We have faith
- ✓ We have hope
- ✓ We know who we are . . . and we act like it
- ✓ We do our very best to cultivate compassion, courage, creativity, and authenticity
- ✓ We are kind
- ✓ We embrace humility . . . and humor
- ✓ We try and try again to believe in optimism as we recognize the importance of love, frienship, loyalty, and connection
- ✓ We work to place love before fear and connection before separateness, while recognizing that fear is part of courage too
- ✓ We choose to be sincere, empathetic, motivated, perseverant, engaged and excited, and resilient, to reflect without ruminating,

And then Just Roll With It!

# AFTERWORD

Sarah Plummer Taylor's idea of *rolling* resonates favorably with me. I find wisdom in it. In one sense, I could frame my entire life as the extended process of developing my ability to *roll*. Long before I came to know about her and her unique program, I had internalized the concept as a basic life skill.

As captain of the football team and a stand-out defensive player at my college, I learned the importance of *rolling*. When I collided with an opposing lineman and was knocked off balance, for example, I learned to minimize the impact by *rolling*. And when someone hit me hard to take me out, I learned how to *roll* off the forward momentum of the oncoming player and spin around to keep going. *Rolling* was a basic ingredient in learning to play—and survive—the game.

At The University of Alabama where I teach, members of the football team spend quality practice time learning to *roll* downfield toward the end zone. They seek to uphold a reputation built on the value of forward momentum, and they have enjoyed many victorious seasons because of their adherence to it. So important is this and so successfully has this worked for Alabama, that the university has licensed *Roll Tide!* as its official rally chant. It is much more than a college pep rally chant, however. It connotes a way of life.

Soccer, dancing, martial arts, kayaking, and skydiving are a few of the many sports that also teach the worth of *rolling* for maximizing the safety and enjoyment of participants. In such sports, *rolling* serves a profitable twofold function. It simultaneously (1) helps to minimize the possibility of injury, thus enhancing personal effectiveness; and (2) enables a quicker recovery, or turnaround, thus protecting the valuable commodity of time.

Sarah Plummer Taylor's story in the book you have just read is a primer in the art and discipline of *rolling*. Her SEMPER program provides a concrete, specific way to learn how to *roll*. Her techniques are actually customized hand tools for carving out a larger perspective that includes the fashioning of new mental models. Coupled with her questions for self-assessment and her selected quotations from the experience of others, she marks a trail we can follow as we journey toward personal transformation and growth.

Like Sarah Plummer Taylor, *rolling* has played a significant part in my own life story as well. As I learned to face the multidimensional challenges of making my way in the world, *rolling* emerged as an essential way of coping.

Before I ever knew what to call it, I was *rolling* my way forward through the seasons of my life, running downfield, meeting whatever life sent my way and dealing with it the best I could. I *rolled* with adolescence, the divorce of my parents, living on my own in mainland China for a year plus, a life-changing injury during my service in the military, navigating the academic world, and negotiating the worry and wonder of marriage and the parenting of our four wonderful daughters.

Today I am engaged in a relativity new aspect of social work known as military social work. With the massive deployments of the past decade and a half, there is great need for working with service members, veterans, and their families—and with the leaders and resources of the communities to which they return.

Some of America's "wounded warriors" come home with injuries and lifelong disabilities sustained in combat. All of them return seeking to reenter the mainstream of the world they left behind. They hope to find loved ones, jobs, and community support waiting for them.

These warriors also return bearing, in one way or another, the fallout—the brutal physical and emotional scars—of having participated in some fashion in war. They carry their wounds back to the arms of their waiting loved ones and communities. The trauma this creates for them and for their families—and sometimes for their communities— is immense. Its scope is not yet fully appreciated, despite often heroic efforts to reach a helping hand to these veterans and their loved ones. They need understanding and moral support—lots of it—as well as health care and jobs.

Part of what I teach my students is how to care for these human beings who happen to be military veterans and families, and how their real human need can be interfaced with real community resources. As a means to this end, I work to instill in my students the tremendous value of *rolling* for the practice of social work.

Future social workers in this field must learn to "*roll* with it" in their private lives, perhaps by way of a program like Sarah Plummer Taylor's. How can they care for others without such fundamental and ongoing self-care?

But as important as it is, self-care is just the first step. *Rolling* never happens in a vacuum. It presupposes a world of others with whom we must interact in a variety of ways. A few words describe the dynamic here: reentry, integration, assimilation.

To get the job done, those who do military social work must operate from a deep commitment to a form of *rolling* I like to call networking. Because of the vital importance of the civilian community for returning veterans and their families, we teach future military social workers how to "*roll* with" the social structures of our society and its multicultural communities. *Rolling* recognizes and values the power created when there is a convergence of diverse voices to find appropriate solutions.

This means that as professional caregivers, they must devote prime time and energy to encouraging their constituencies—that is, community stakeholders, institutional staff and clients, and others—to develop the life skills that are packaged in the deceptively simple little word *rolling*. Deceptively simple, but incredibly important.

This is why, in teaching military social work, we spend quality "practice time" learning to understand the psychodynamics of such things as resiliency and strengths-based approaches to care. These are, after all, the theoretical components of *rolling* that comprise the practical effort required to put *rolling* into successful practice. It takes both to achieve a successful outcome by any measure.

*Rolling* does not mean to "settle." It is not a retreat from adversity, danger, or conflict. On the contrary, *rolling* is a way to meet and move through the chances and changes of life, whether illness, setbacks, loss, or even success. It is not merely a survival skill, though it is that. It is, more significantly, a means to thrive.

*Rolling* can be thought of in many ways. It resonates on both individual and societal levels. What Joe Batten famously said in his advertising slogan developed for the United States Army a number of years ago best articulates its purpose: "Be All You Can Be!"

I am grateful to Sarah Plummer Taylor for seeing the central importance of *"rolling* with it." I salute her and those like her, military and civilian alike, who are rising to the challenge of *rolling*. They and others like them are about something vitally important to our national security, our economic sustainability, and our common welfare—all of which make possible the pursuit of happiness.

**—David L. Albright, PhD**

Dr. Albright is an associate professor and Hill Crest Foundation Endowed Chair in Mental Health at The University of Alabama in Tuscaloosa, Alabama, USA. He is available for consultation, speaking, and workshops, and can be contacted at dlalbright@ua.edu.

# ENDNOTES

**Chapter 9**

1. The flight, fight, or freeze response as well as alterations of consciousness and dissociative states are well documented in the trauma literature and research, especially in regards to rape victims' experiences. Judith Herman, Trauma and Recovery: The aftermath of violence—from domestic abuse to political terror (MD Basic Books ©1992, 1997) p42–43.

2. Some college campuses have recently (as of 2015) implemented a guilty caller policy where a local police department is allowed to listen to a call if a victim is willing to call their attacker. With alarming regularity, the attacker confesses. Then that confession can be used in future legal proceedings.

# APPENDIX 1—SMOOTHIE RECIPES

## CHOCOLATE STRAWBERRY SUPER-SMOOTHIE RECIPE

We know that all berries are rich in antioxidants. Here is a pleasant surprise for you, though: the #1 antioxidant rich food is *chocolate*! Yes, CHOCOLATE! Real chocolate, not Snickers or M&M's, contains fifteen times more antioxidants than blueberries, twenty times more than green tea, and thirty times more than red wine. Beyond just recognizing the antioxidant level within the food, we also want to know how much of it actually even makes it into our bloodstream. That's why it is helpful to know that when you mix berries and chocolate together, their antioxidant power blasts off like Superman and is magnified the way it is because it is increasing the bioavailability of those antioxidants by two or three times their normal amount. Get some superfood chocolate and berries into your bloodstream!

If you don't have a VitaMix, start saving for one. It's the most glorious invention ever. On the other hand, if you only have a sad, sad blender, go ahead and use that.

Combine ingredients in this order:

1 cup clean water
1/2–1 tbs coconut oil (long chain (a.k.a. good for you) fat. We need fats for neurological health!)
1/2 cup Greek yogurt (small amounts of high quality dairy are okay for many of us)
1/4 cup macadamia nuts
1 scoop of YOR Health Supergreens powder
1 tsp of Nutrex pacifca spirulina (even though the YOR Health Supergreens has some spirulina in it, we love the health benefits and always add more separately)
1 tbs organic local honey (Honey is the #1 enzyme food out there as well as a *prana* concentrator because it involves all forms of energy from the ground up (the soil grows the flowers, the bees get the pollen

from the flowers, convert into honey goodness, etc.). Also, honey is a great source of trace minerals.)

1 tbs maca powder (an adaptagenic root known for its dynamic effects of boosting energy, relieving stress, and increasing libido. Hey-ooooh!)

1/4 cup cacao nibs (a.k.a. real chocolate)

1 1/2cups frozen strawberries

3 big leaves of kale, or a handful or two of spinach

Then, make sure lid is on tight.

Blend.

Pour.

Drink.

Smile.

## PETE'S GREAT GREEN SMOOTHIE RECIPE

1 1/2 cups liquid (water or almond milk suggested)

1/2 to 3/4 of a cucumber

2 stalks of celery

1/2 pear

1 banana

3–4 leaves of kale

1 leaf of chard

One knuckle of ginger root

1 tbs each of chia seeds, hemp hearts, and honey

*Be sure to sign up for my free e-newsletter at www.SemperSarah.com because I frequently cover nutritional issues and provide quick and easy healthy recipes to get you rolling in the right direction!*

# APPENDIX 2—SUGGESTED READING

**FAITH**

*The Celestine Prophecy*
*Searching For God Knows What*
*The Language of God*

**SINCERITY**

*Blink*
*The Alchemist*
*The Gifts of Imperfection*

**EMPATHY**

*Rule Number Two*
*The Glass Castle*
*My Sister's Keeper*

**MOTIVATION**

*Thrive: The Vegan Nutrition Guide to Optimal Performance*
*The Purpose-Driven Life*

**PERSEVERANCE**

*Seabiscuit*
*The Art of Racing in the Rain*

**ENGAGEMENT AND EXCITEMENT**

*The Charge*
*Born To Run*
*Eiger Dreams*

## RESILIENCE

*Anatomy of the Spirit*
*The Body Keeps the Score*

## JRWI

*Brave, Strong, and True: The Modern Warrior's Battle for Balance*
*Happy Yoga*

These are some of my all-time favorite books. Many could fall into several of the SEMPER categories. Read one and let me know what you think. I'd love to hear from you! Post a comment about these books and how they relate to one, or many, of the SEMPER traits on my Facebook page—www.Facebook.com/SemperSarah

# FURTHER RESOURCES

To contact Sarah for select speaking engagements, please visit www.SemperSarah.com/speaking

To get Sarah Plummer Taylor's FREE e-newsletter and a simple yet powerful breathwork guide just for signing up, visit her website: www.SemperSarah.com

Sarah Plummer Taylor's blog: www.SemperSarah.com/blog

"Semper Sarah" Plummer Taylor on Facebook: www.Facebook.com/SemperSarah

Sarah Plummer Taylor on Twitter: @Semper_Sarah

Sarah Plummer Taylor's international retreats: www.SemperSarah.com/Retreat

To learn more about the training, education, and programs offered by Just Roll With It Wellness, please visit www.JustRollWithItWellness.com

# REFERENCE LIST OF QUOTES

## CHAPTER 2—ROLLING WITH WHAT? WHAT IS SEMPER?

1. Chödrön, Pema. 2004. *Start Where You Are: A Guide to Compassionate Living.* Boston: Shambala.
   "Everything is changing all the time, and we keep wanting to pin it down, to fix it. So whenever you come up with a solid conclusion, let the rug be pulled out. You can pull out your own rug, and you can also let life pull it out for you. . . . One way to pull out your own rug is by just letting go, lightening up, being more gentle, and not making such a big deal."

2. The Big Apple. Entry from December 18, 2002. Chinese Proverb. "Teachers open the door, but you must enter by yourself."
   http://www.barrypopik.com/index.php/new_york_city/entry/teachers_open_the_door_but_you_must_enter_by_yourself

3. Gaiam Life. Marianne Williamson quote. "Know that there's room for everyone to be passionate, creative and successful. In fact, there's more than room for everyone; there's a need for everyone."
   http://blog.gaiam.com/quotes/authors/marianne-williamson/60619

4. Goodreads. Nikos Kazantzakis quotes. "True teachers are those who use themselves as bridges over which they invite their students to cross; then, having facilitated their crossing, joyfully collapse, encouraging them to create their own."
   http://www.goodreads.com/quotes/241321-true-teachers-are-those-who-use-themselves-as-bridges-over

5. Ross, Steve. 2003. *Happy Yoga.* New York: Harper.
   "Trying to make what is temporary last only causes distress. Yes, change upsets the illusion of psychological security. You can either agonize over this and fight it fruitlessly, or you can choose to pierce through the illusion to the truth. When

you start coming from a place of acceptance rather than the standard, chronic state of resistant, nonacceptance, your experience of life cannot be stopped from totally changing for the better. Happiness is a function of acceptance."

6. Andrew Himes blog. David Orr quote. "The planet does not need more 'successful' people. But it does desperately need more peacemakers, healers, restorers, storytellers, and lovers of every shape and form. It needs people who live well in their places. It needs people of moral courage willing to join the fight to make the world habitable and humane. And these needs have little to do with success as our culture has defined it."

   http://andrewhimes.net/node/742

7. Values.com. Author unknown. "Peace. It doesn't mean to be in a place where there is no noise, trouble, or hard work. It means to be in the midst of those things and still be calm in your heart."

   http://www.values.com/inspirational-quotes/7228-peace-it-does-not-mean-to-be-in-a-place-where

8. Instagram. Quote by Vivian Greene. "Life is not about waiting for the storm to pass…it's about learning to dance in the rain."
   https://instagram.com/p/7sxKtlkMK2/?taken-by=dancingqueen_ox

9. Facebook. "Higher Perspectives" page. Daniel Saint quote. "If you wish to be a warrior prepare to get broken, if you wish to be an explorer prepare to get lost, and if you wish to be a lover prepare to be both."
   https://www.facebook.com/HigherPerspective/photos/a.488358504529807.114722.488353241197000/1019276134771372/

10. Goodreads. Jan Glidewell quote. "You can clutch your past so tightly to your chest that it leaves your arms too full to embrace the present."
    http://www.goodreads.com/quotes/432910-you-can-clutch-the-past-so-tightly-to-your-chest

## CHAPTER 3—FAITH

1.  Brown, Brené. 2010. *The Gifts of Imperfection.* Center City, MN: Hazelden.
    "It seems that gratitude without practice may be a little like faith without works—it's not alive."
2.  Yamada, Kobi. "She" as found in *Happy Yoga* by Steve Ross. 2003. New York: Harper. "She went out on a limb, had it break off behind her, and discovered she could fly."
3.  Myss, Carolyn. 1996. *Anatomy of the Spirit.* New York: Harmony.
4.  Goodreads. Norman B. Rice quote. "Dare to reach out your hand into the darkness, to pull another hand into the light." https://www.goodreads.com/quotes/779001-dare-to-reach-out-your-hand-into-the-darkness-to

## CHAPTER 4—SINCERE

1.  Ignited Quotes. "Quotes about being yourself." Lao-tzu. "When you are content simply to be yourself and don't compare or compete, everyone will respect you." http://www.ignitedquotes.com/quotes-about-being-yourself
2.  Frederick Buechner, as quoted by my personal spiritual mentor, Dr. Lainie Allen. "This side of Paradise, it is our business (not, like so many, peddlers of God's word but as men and women of sincerity) to speak with our hearts (which is what sincerity means) and to bear witness to, and live out of, and live toward, and live by, the true word of His holy story as it seeks to stammer itself forth through the holy stories of us all."
3.  Wise Quotes. Henry David Thoreau. "What a man thinks of himself, that is which determines, or rather indicates, his fate." http://wise-quotes.net/dnv5h/
4.  What Christians Want to Know. "25 Inspirational Ralph Waldo Emerson Quotes." "The only relationship you can control is the one with yourself. What lies behind us, and what lies before us, are tiny matters when compared to what lies within us." http://www.whatchristianswanttoknow.com/25-inspirational-ralph-waldo-emerson-quotes/

5.  Beal, Kris M. The Heart & Humor of Being Human. "The Messy Side of Being Brave."
    http://www.krismbeal.com/2015/09/19/brave/

6.  College Street Journal. Anna Quindlen. "The thing that is really hard, and really amazing, is giving up on being perfect and beginning the work of becoming yourself."
    https://www.mtholyoke.edu/offices/comm/csj/990604/Quindlen.html

7.  Writing the Energetic Body. "Chakra Quotes." Bhagwan Shree Rajne. "The moment you accept yourself as you are, all burdens, mountainous burdens simply disappear. Then life is a sheer joy."
    https://writingtheenergeticbody.wordpress.com/quotes/1st-chakra/

8.  Covey, Stephen R. 1989. *The 7 Habits of Highly Effective People*. New York: Free Press.
    "If I really want to improve my situation, I can work on the one thing over which I have control—myself."

## CHAPTER 5—EMPATHETIC

1.  Clark, M. J., MA, APR. 2011. *Shut Up and Lead*. Columbus, OH: M. J. Clark, MA, APR.
    "Letting someone know you understand the feeling he or she is experiencing is powerful, even if you can't say you have had the same experience. It's the empathy that counts."

2.  Pinterest. Elisabeth Kübler-Ross. "The most beautiful people we have known are those who have known defeat, known suffering, known struggle, known loss, and have found their way out of the depths. These persons have an appreciation, a sensitivity, and an understanding of life that fills them with compassion, gentleness, and a deep loving concern. Beautiful people do not just happen."
    https://www.pinterest.com/pin/369084131933400629/

3.  Bonhoeffer, Dietrich. 1997. *Letters and Papers from Prison*. New York: Touchstone.

"We must learn to regard people less in the light of what they do or omit to do, and more in the light of what they suffer."

4.  Goodreads. Gillian Deacon quote. "There is no prescription for finding moments of gratitude in every day; there is simply the choice."
    https://www.goodreads.com/author/quotes/1421938.
    Gillian_Deacon

5.  Burchard, Brendon. 2012. *The Charge: Activating the 10 Human Drives That Make You Feel Alive.* New York: Free Press.
    "By reengaging people with their emotions, therapists help people find a greater sense of self-care and empathy for others."

6.  Miller, William R. and Stephen Rollnick. 2013. *Motivational Interviewing: Helping People Change.* New York: The Guilford Press.
    Carl R. Rogers: "It is astonishing how elements that seem insoluable become soluable when someone listens, how confusions that seem irremediable turn into relatively clear flowing streams when one is heard. I have deeply appreciated the times that I have experienced this sensitive, empathic, concentrated listening."

## CHAPTER 6—MOTIVATED

1.  Anderson, Mac. 2008. *Charging the Human Battery: 50 Ways to Motivate Yourself.* Naperville, IL: Simple Truths.
    John Blumberg: "Motives are like the rudder of a boat. The motor moves the boat, but if the rudder is just slightly set at the wrong angle . . . well, you can end up in the wrong place."

2.  Goodreads. Lou Holtz quote. "Ability is what you're capable of doing. Motivation determines what you do. Attitude determines how well you do it."
    http://www.goodreads.com/author/show/85179.Lou_Holtz

3.  Goodreads. Stephen Covey. "Individuals can affect the world by becoming a model or an example in their small circle of

influence. Just as a rock thrown into a pond causes ripples to gradually keep going out until eventually they are very small, so our acts influence the ecology of the entire human race." https://www.goodreads.com/author/quotes/1538. Stephen_R_Covey?page=2

4. BrainyQuote. Bo Bennet quote. "A dream becomes a goal when action is taken toward its achievement." http://www.brainyquote.com/quotes/quotes/b/bobennett167540.html

5. Values.com. Inspirational quotes. Martin Luther King, Jr. "Everybody can be great because anybody can serve. You only need a heart full of grace, a soul generated by love." http://www.values.com/inspirational-quotes/5089-everybody-can-be-great-because-anybody-can

6. Quotes.net. Robert F. Kennedy. "Each time a person stands up for an ideal, or acts to improve the lot of others, or strikes out against injustice, he sends forth a tiny ripple of hope, and crossing each other from a million different centers of energy and daring, these ripples build a current that can sweep down the mightiest walls of oppression and resistance." http://www.quotes.net/quote/4999

7. Goodreads. Mark Twain quote. "Keep away from people who try to belittle your ambitions. Small people always do that, but the really great make you feel that you, too, can become great." https://www.goodreads.com/quotes/2528-keep-away-from-people-who-try-to-belittle-your-ambitions

## CHAPTER 7—PERSEVERANT

8. Anderson, Mac. 2008. *Charging the Human Battery: 50 Ways to Motivate Yourself.* Naperville, IL: Simple Truths.
Henry Ford: "Failure is the only opportunity to begin again more intelligently."

9. Miller, William R. and Stephen Rollnick. 2013. *Motivational Interviewing: Helping People Change.* New York: The Guilford Press.

Albert Einstein: "Out of clutter, find simplicity. From discord, find harmony. In the middle of difficulty lies opportunity."

10. Goodreads. John Wooden quotes. "Never try to be better than someone else. But never stop working to become your best self."
http://www.goodreads.com/quotes/234201-never-try-to-be-better-than-someone-else-learn-from

11. Van Dernoot Lipsky, Laura with Connie Burk. 2009. *Trauma Stewardship: An Everyday Guide to Caring for Self While Caring for Others.* San Francisco: Berrett-Koehler Publishers, Inc.
Chinese proverb as seen in source: "You can only go halfway into the darkest forest; then you're coming out the other side."

12. BrainyQuote. Winston Churchill. "If you're going through hell, keep going."
http://www.brainyquote.com/quotes/quotes/w/winstonchu103788.html

13. BrainyQuote. Georgia O'Keeffe. "I've been absolutely terrified every moment of my life—and I've never let it keep me from doing a single thing I wanted to do."
http://www.brainyquote.com/quotes/authors/g/georgia_okeeffe.html

14. Goodreads. Martin Luther King, Jr. quotes. "If you can't fly then run, if you can't run then walk, if you can't walk then crawl, but whatever you do you have to keep moving forward."
http://www.goodreads.com/quotes/26963-if-you-can-t-fly-then-run-if-you-can-t-run

15. Goodreads. George Mueller quotes. "To learn strong faith is to endure great trials. I have learned my faith by standing firm amid severe testings."
http://www.goodreads.com/quotes/1232524-the-only-way-to-learn-strong-faith-is-to-endure

## CHAPTER 8—ENGAGED AND EXCITED

1. Goodreads. Ralph Waldo Emerson quotes. "Enthusiasm is one of the most powerful engines of success. When you do

a thing, do it with all your might. Put your whole soul into it. Stamp it with your own personality. Be active, be energetic, be enthusiastic and faithful, and you will accomplish your object. Nothing great was ever achieved without enthusiasm." http://www.goodreads.com/author/show/12080.Ralph_ Waldo_Emerson_

2. Dalai Lama. 1998. *The Art of Happiness.* New York: Simon & Schuster.
   "The purpose in life is to be happy."

3. Miller, William R. and Stephen Rollnick. 2013. *Motivational Interviewing: Helping People Change.* New York: The Guilford Press.
   Carl Sandburg: "Alike and ever alike we are on all continents in need of love, food, clothing, work, speech, worship, sleep, games, dancing, fun. From tropics to arctics humanity lives with these needs so alike, so inexorably alike."

4. Anderson, Mac. 2008. *Charging the Human Battery: 50 Ways to Motivate Yourself.* Naperville, IL: Simple Truths.
   Plato: "Life must be lived as play."

5. Hendricks Thomas, Kate. 2015. *Brave, Strong, and True: The Modern Warrior's Battle for Balance.* Collierville, TN: Innovo Publishing LLC. (excerpt)

6. Hayhouse Radio. Robert Holden. "People who follow their joy discover a depth of creativity and talent that inspires the world."
   http://www.hhemarketing.com/author/holden/ppl/ppl_ holden_event2-3_041509.html

7. Anderson, Mac. 2008. *Charging the Human Battery: 50 Ways to Motivate Yourself.* Naperville IL: Simple Truths.
   Bill Meyer: "Every thought is a seed. If you plant crab apples, don't count on harvesting golden delicious."

## CHAPTER 9—RESILIENT

1. Pinterest. Elizabeth Kübler-Ross quote. "The most beautiful people we have known are those who have known defeat,

known suffering, known struggle, known loss, and have found their way out of the depths. These persons have an appreciation, a sensitivity, and an understanding of life that fills them with compassion, gentleness, and a deep loving concern. Beautiful people do not just happen."
https://www.pinterest.com/pin/369084131933400629/

2.  Values.com. Inspirational quotes. Buddha. "Holding onto anger is like holding on to a hot coal with the intent of throwing it at someone else; you are the one who gets burned."
http://www.values.com/inspirational-quotes/6683-holding-on-to-anger-is-like-grasping-a-hot-coal

3.  Goodreads. Fred Devito quotes. "If it doesn't challenge you, it doesn't change you."
http://www.goodreads.com/quotes/646638-if-it-doesn-t-challenge-you-it-doesn-t-change-you

4.  Dribben, Melissa. 2011. "Silent fight: Sex assault against servicewomen." *The News and Observer*, Chapel Hill, Sept.18, p. 19A.

5.  Anderson, Mac. 2008. *Charging the Human Battery: 50 Ways to Motivate Yourself*. Naperville IL: Simple Truths.
Abraham Lincoln: "Most people are about as happy as they make up their minds to be."

6.  Goodreads. Tony Robbins quotes. "Identify your problems, but give your power and energy to solutions."
http://www.goodreads.com/quotes/5136-identify-your-problems-but-give-your-power-and-energy-to

7.  Coelho, Paulo. 1993. *The Alchemist*. New York: Harper Collins. "No matter what he does, every person on earth plays a central role in the history of the world. And normally he doesn't know it."

8.  George Carlin as cited in *Happy Yoga* by Steve Ross. 2003. New York: Harper. "Don't sweat the petty things, and don't pet the sweaty things."

9.  Facebook. Agni. "Certainty comes by using your gifts, by allowing your power to change your world. Forgiveness of your own past is the starter and then work with all your love."

https://www.facebook.com/permalink.php?story_fbid
=10150835314446616&id=128842836615&comment_
id=22100023&offset=0&total_comment

10. BeyondPregnancyLoss.com. 30 Steps Toward Healing. Cat Forsley. "What we give our attention to—stays with us. What we let go of—will let go of us."
http://beyondpregnancyloss.com/30-steps-toward-healing/
step-20-letting-go/

11. Scrapbook.com. Resources. Quotes. Life Experiences. Alan Cohen. "It takes a lot of courage to release the familiar and seemingly secure, to embrace the new. But there is no real security in what is no longer meaningful. There is more security in the adventurous and exciting, for in movement there is life, and in change there is power."
http://www.scrapbook.com/quotes/doc/25153.html

12. Chödrön, Pema. 2000. *When Things Fall Apart: Heart Advice for Difficult Times*. Boston: Shambhala Classics.
"Only to the extent that we expose ourselves over and over to annihilation can that which is indestructible in us be found."

13. My Yoga Tutor. Blogs. BKS Iyengar."Health is a state of complete harmony of the body, mind and spirit. When one is free from physical disabilities and mental distractions, the gates of the soul open."
http://myyogatutor.com/santosha/2979/

14. Ross, Steve. 2003. *Happy Yoga*. New York: Harper.
"Spiritual life is like a medicinal herb: bitter in the beginning, sweet in the end. Becoming conscious can initially be challenging. But once you get rolling, your life becomes peaceful, blissful, and much sweeter for your efforts."

15. Goodreads. Albert Einstein quotes. "In the middle of difficulty lies opportunity."
http://www.goodreads.com/quotes/7275-in-the-middle-of-
difficulty-lies-opportunity

16. BrainyQuote. Robert Frost. "In three words I can sum up everything I've learned about life. It goes on."
http://www.brainyquote.com/quotes/quotes/r/
robertfros101059.html

## CONCLUSION: JUST ROLL WITH IT

1.  Miller, Donald. 2005. *Through Painted Deserts*. Nashville, TN: Nelson Books.
    "I want to keep my soul fertile for the changes, so things keep getting born in me, so things keep dying when it is time for things to die. I want to keep walking away from the person I was a moment ago, because a mind was made to figure things out, not to read the same page recurrently."

2.  Pinterest. Deepak Chopra. "Holding on to anything is like holding on to your breath. You will suffocate. The only way to get anything in the physical universe is by letting go of it. Let go and it will be yours forever."
    https://www.pinterest.com/pin/127297126938967744/

3.  Myss, Carolyn. 1996. *Anatomy of the Spirit*. New York: Three Rivers Press.
    "You will only be sent more and more teachers, each more intense than the previous one. Your task is to learn the lesson that the teacher has for you rather than to resent the teacher."

4.  Miller, Donald. 2005. *Through Painted Deserts*. Nashville TN: Nelson Books.
    "Everybody has to change, or they expire."

5.  Quote.place. Mark Batterson. "Embrace relational uncertainty. It's called romance. Embrace spiritual uncertainty. It's called mystery. Embrace occupational uncertainty. It's called destiny. Embrace emotional uncertainty. It's called joy. Embrace intellectual uncertainty. It's called revelation."
    http://quotes.place/quote-31599/

6.  Carlson, Kristine. 2001. *Don't Sweat the Small Stuff for Women*. New York: Hyperion.
    "As you begin to see the twists and turns—those surprising events and circumstances that happen for a reason you are not yet aware of—you'll realize that everything that happens to you is part of a perfect plan designed especially for your personalized, Life 101 course."

7.  Goodreads. Steve Jobs quotes. "Your time is limited, so don't waste it living someone else's life. Don't be trapped by dogma—

which is living with the results of other people's thinking. Don't let the noise of other's opinions drown out your own inner voice. And most importantly, have the courage to follow your heart and intuition. They somehow already know what you truly want to become. Everything else is secondary."
http://www.goodreads.com/author/quotes/5255891.Steve_ Jobs

8.  Carlson, Dr. Richard. 1997. *Don't Sweat the Small Stuff . . . and it's all small stuff!* New York: Hyperion.
    "Take the focus off yourself and imagine what it's like to be in someone else's predicament, and simultaneously feel love for that person. It's the recognition that other people's problems, their pain and frustrations, are every bit as real as our own—often far worse."

9.  Neil, Terry. 2008. *Charging the Human Battery: 50 Ways to Motivate Yourself.* Naperville IL: Simple Truths.
    "Courage is a door that can only be opened from the inside."

10. BrainyQuote. Eleanor Roosevelt. "We must do the things we think we cannot do."
    http://www.brainyquote.com/quotes/authors/e/eleanor_roosevelt.html

11. Goodreads. Albert Camus quotes. "When you have once seen the glow of happiness on the face of a beloved person, you know that a man can have no vocation but to awaken that light on the faces surrounding him. In the depth of winter, I finally learned that within me there lay an invincible summer."
    http://www.goodreads.com/quotes/226128-when-you-have-once-seen-the-glow-of-happiness-on

12. Goodreads. Voltaire quotes. "I have chosen to be happy because it is good for my health."
    http://www.goodreads.com/quotes/583598-i-have-chosen-to-be-happy-because-it-is-good

13. Goodreads. Socrates quotes. "Let him who would move the world, first move himself."
    http://www.goodreads.com/quotes/23687-let-him-who-would-move-the-world-first-move-himself

14. Positively Positive. Karen Salmansohn. "The first step to living the life you want is leaving the life you don't want. Taking the first step forward is always the hardest, but then each step forward gets easier and easier and each step forward gets you closer and closer until eventually what had once been invisible starts to be visible, and what had once felt impossible starts to feel possible."
http://www.positivelypositive.com/2012/07/06/the-first-step-to-living-the-life-you-want/

15. We're So Inspired. Success. "This is to Have Succeeded." Ralph Waldo Emerson. "To know that even one life has breathed easier because you have lived, that is to have succeeded."
http://weresoinspired.com/this-is-to-have-succeeded/#.VfypAOtDkTs

16. Pitchford, Paul, MS. 2007. *Integrative Nutrition: Feed Your Hunger for Health & Happiness.* Austin, TX: Greenleaf Book Group "Simply being more aware of imbalance is the first step to becoming more balanced."

# ACKNOWLEDGMENTS

Putting gratitude down in static form on these pages is perhaps one of the most difficult tasks in completing this work. There are more people to thank and in ways that I feel inadequate to do by written word alone, but I will do my best.

First and foremost, I really do thank our beautiful, mysterious, and loving God in all the forms God takes. My life would not be what it is today if not for the gifts, grace, and Divine mercy I've experienced firsthand. Thank You, Lord, for picking me up and piecing me back together again when the time called for it. Most of all, where I've witnessed Your presence most powerfully is among the people in my life, and for all of them, thank You a thousand times over.

Pete, your name is incredibly apropos since you are my rock. "Thank you" will never sufficiently express the appreciation I have for the positive impact you've made on my life, the peace and safety you bring into my world, the unyielding reassurance you've offered, and the patience you've displayed. You have loved me, nourished me, forgiven me, held me, challenged me, accepted me as I am, and loved me all over again. For that and so much more, I love you.

Mom and Dad, my first two teachers, thank you. Although neither of you were ever officially my coach or teacher, you taught me so much on and off the field, track, and court, and in and out of the pool and classroom, and continue to do so to this day. I love you both so much. Thank you for every lap you made me run, every drill you made me do, every book report you made me write, and all the advice you gave. You always thought the best of me and you never let me quit. I kept moving forward in life because of your encouragement, humility, and dedication to self-improvement. Mom, specifically thank you for your edits on the previous editions of this manuscript. Dad, thank you for your unfailing love and positivity around all my work, difficult and otherwise. We are all so painfully imperfect, but that's what makes us the family we are. Thank God there were so many cracks in us all so the light could get in.

Becci, sister, friend, partner in crime, hilarious, creative, brilliant, beautiful being, I love you. Your impact on my life is immeasurable and we share the bond that only sisters do that's got tons of fun, buckets of tears (both happy and sad), world travels memories, family analysis, hurts and truths, shared battles, inside jokes, secrets, and support. My heart is as big as it is because of you. Thank you.

Grammy Mickie, I know you're here by my side on this journey. You really were the example to all of us in so many ways. You showed us how to love despite deep wounds, how to adapt and overcome, how to stay kind, compassionate, and creative as your years marched on. You gave the best back scratches and told the most interesting family adventure stories while doing so. I miss you every day. Thank you for the light you shone on my life for so long.

Karen, Larry and Sharon, Chris and Kristy, and Kate and Tim, how blessed I consider myself to now call you family too. Each of you shows me more and more how love can look. I am so grateful for inclusion in your clan.

I have a deep sense of gratitude toward more people than I could name here, and even names I likely do not know, but people who have touched my life in striking ways. Specifically, I must give great thanks to some of my most beloved friends and partners though.

Kate, it's been seventeen years of friendship now. Holy cow—we're getting old! From UVA and our early days in Air Force ROTC, to Marine Corps ROTC moto kitties throwing ourselves over rough obstacles and similarly featured relationships, DC trouble making and life-guarding good old days, sisters-in-arms, supporters on deployments, to growing up strong and becoming creative partners and "perfect friends" (to steal your Aristotle reference), we've seen a lot together. I especially appreciate your thoughtful feedback, respect, encouragement, worst-case-scenario'ing-it, laughing, crying, calling to talk about work and ending up talking about life, and inspiration you add to my days. Thank you for being real, for being my "inconveniently godly" friend.

Margie oh "Largie," now sixteen years of friendship and I'm afraid we are more preposterous than ever before! Wind us up and let us loose! You are the best friend, travel, and yoga and soccer soulmate a girl could ever ask for. You are probably the first person who really taught me how to "just roll with it" without even realizing that I was your student. You are both a peer and "roll" model to me. I miss our *center-middy* days at UVA so badly. During those times, I equally cherished our friendship and admired your composure on the field, and your ridiculousness off of it. We always have a "blasty" together, no matter where in the world we may be or what adventure we may be up to. I so love how our friendship has continued to evolve as we have, and it's an honor to call you my "bestie." Love you deeply, Largie.

Lainie and Daniel, God blessed me with you two, that is for sure! Having met you both at the beginning of my walk with Christ and continuing to have you by my side—and then Pete's and my side—throughout the years is Divine handiwork worth celebrating. Hallelujah!

Lisa, trusty goddess, conduit of yogic wisdom, friendship, love, and light, you too are a beautiful gift to this world and one who has made immeasurable impacts of grace, love, peace, patience, wisdom, and growth upon my life. Namaste, my friend.

The Freyja Project and lovely, light being and leader, Patty; teacher-friends; students; *kula* and *sangha*, I am so grateful for you all and for how you make a rootless child feel at home in Denver.

Veterans of Foreign Wars Post-1, and Michael Mitchel and John Keene, specifically, thank you so much for facilitating creative and dynamic approaches to support and serve our nation's veterans as well as giving me a place to teach something I cherish to people about whom I deeply care. Team Red White and Blue, Mike Erwin, Steve and Megan, Chris Widell, Mark Erwin, thank you for your support in the early days and beyond; Service Women's Action Network for your rocking social justice impacts; and Anu Bhagwati, what an honor to call you a friend and confidant; The Giveback Yoga Foundation, Rob Schware, Shanti Medina, thank you for your service-oriented hearts and the love and support you've provided; Comeback Yoga, Margot, and Ned you are bright lights in this community; huge hugs and gratitude to all of you and to each of your organizations.

Bart and Darya at Innovo Publishing, our work together has reignited my relationship with Christ and provided a platform to live my mission. Thanks certainly is not enough to express my gratefulness for the role you've played in that.

215

Lydia, thank you for your countless hours and our evolving sisterhood; I trust your input and insights implicitly. Your hand and heart have touched all elements of my work the past couple of years and subsequently the lives of so many others. Keep doing you; it's incredible! I extend a massive thank you to you from my heart to yours.

There are so many people I want and need to thank at great length. These are people who have supported me, pushed me, loved me, and taught me life lessons. They have also made me laugh, cry, and everything in between! These special people include, but are not limited to, my amazing friend Leigh who inspires me to be a kind, bold, and beautiful momma and friend; my brother, Matt; my sister, Rachel; my aunt Sandi and cousin Tom; my grandmother Elizabeth who is not with us anymore; my uncle Robert; some of my very first mentors and spiritual guides, Nathalie and Paul Sarigianis, and Blaire Cholewa, as well as many others who have made huge impacts on my soul walk; Theresa Larrey and our San Diego small group, Ana LaNave, and my St. Charles Landings small group in Arlington, VA; my saviors in a barren land, Doctors Matt Davis and Ivy Hambrick; my dear friends, Caitlin and Clem Spriggs, Mama Theis, Francisco and Megan Tataje, Dan Stover, Christy Little, Cindy and Dan Hamilton, Tori Jensen, Bryan Sargent; soccer gal pals too numerous to name but certainly BG's Haley and Jamie, Britt, Mindy, Nora; Auggie and Dale; sports friends like Alan Gardner (brother!), Adam Kiefert, Brit Davies, Chet Ridenour, John "Fish" Fisher; the DU Women's Club Soccer Team and Meg in particular; old friends and people I love dearly like Megan Luczko, Matt Hilton, D. J. Fuller, Ken Curtis, Donna Charles, Mike Bergen, Tim Bertocci, Christy Acojedo, Laura and Dan, and Mike and Celese Stevens; new friends encountered along the entrepreneur walk like Kristine Carlson, Kristen Moeller, Prescott Paulin, Nathalie Osborn, Danny Brassell, Virginia Barkley, Matt Patterson, Larry Broughton, Jerome Carter, James Malinchak, Steven Diebold, Susan Post, Stephanie Wisdom, M. J. Clark; other friends, mentors, influencers, supporters, and inspirers such as the Wounded Warrior Project and Joe Shearer, Erin Weed, JennJenn Calway, Dan Huvane, Semper Fidelis Health and Wellness, Lindsey Hardman, Vernice Armour, and Betty Moseley Brown. Friends from near and far who encourage me and uplift, Vanessa Bruns Mahoney, Kris Beal, Cara and Karl, Karen Duncan, all of the Columbus

Jackaroos and Jillaroos, the Denver Gaels and Bulldogs, Doug Gertner, Patrick Caffrey, Jennifer Miller; Costa Rica Yoga Spa and Jill Hill, my yoga teachers Marianne and Ron Wells, Ashley Ludman, and Rebecca Kovacs, Sarah Teddy Klein, Becky, and Stephanie from Burn Studio in Columbus OH, YogaPod Lodo in Denver and Rachel and Alex; military mentors like Jill Chambers and Joe Shusko, Colonel Nueman, Dan Deitz, Dan Rodman, Lori Krusulich, Auggie Mendez, Steve Dinote, Chris Steel, Colonel Barraclaugh, and James Kyte. I feel so much gratitude to the University of Denver's Graduate School of Social Work and the teachers and faculty who have so positively impacted my life. Also, special thanks to new mentors such as Dr. David Albright for your insightful afterword and sincere encouragement when I first met you in Alabama and Dr. Charles Hoge for being interested in my work and willing to give me considerate and honest feedback.

Last, but truly not least at all, the sincerest of gratitude from my li'l heart to your big ones—my readers, clients, and students. You have taught me so much; you have shown me real resilience; you have made me laugh; you have inspired others; you have been brave, strong, and true; you have worked hard, loved big, and been courageous. You have Just Rolled With It in more amazing ways than I could've ever imagined. It has been an honor to be your guide in whatever small or big ways I have been. Thank you for being who you are and for letting me into your lives.

# ABOUT THE AUTHOR

Sarah Plummer Taylor, MSW, CHC, is the owner of Semper Sarah®, founder of JRWI Wellness, and co-authored the Just Roll With It Wellness Journal. Sarah received her bachelor's degree from the University of Virginia and her Master's in Social Work from the University of Denver. Previously a captain in the United States Marine Corps and five-time Military Olympic Athlete, today Sarah is an in-demand, international speaker and highly sought-after resiliency coach and trainer, as well as RYT500 Yoga Instructor. She teaches and leads wellness retreats in the US and abroad, and runs a private Holistic Health Counseling practice serving military veterans, professional women, and those seeking to improve all aspects of their health. Sarah has been featured as a lifestyle and wellness expert in *Vanity Fair*, *Marie Claire*, *The New York Times*, *Origin Magazine*, ABC, NBC, and many other national outlets. She lives in Denver with her husband and three-legged wonder dog.